DATE DUE

DEC 1 1 2002	
MAR 1 9 2003	
OCT 0 7 2003	
OCT 1 9 2004	
DEC 0 6 2004	
MAR 1 1 2005	
FEB 1 4 2007	
MAR 1 9 2007	
SEP 2 3 2011	
OCT 1 3 2011	
MAR 0 8 2018	
JUL 2 3 2018	

BRODART, CO.   Cat. No. 23-221-003

THE ENCYCLOPEDIA OF PSYCHOACTIVE DRUGS

SERIES 1

The Addictive Personality
Alcohol and Alcoholism
Alcohol: *Customs and Rituals*
Alcohol: *Teenage Drinking*
Amphetamines: *Danger in the Fast Lane*
Barbiturates: *Sleeping Potions or Intoxicants?*
Caffeine: *The Most Popular Stimulant*
Cocaine: *A New Epidemic*
Escape from Anxiety and Stress
Flowering Plants: *Magic in Bloom*
Getting Help: *Treatments for Drug Abuse*
Heroin: *The Street Narcotic*
Inhalants: *The Toxic Fumes*

LSD: *Visions or Nightmares?*
Marijuana: *Its Effects on Mind & Body*
Methadone: *Treatment for Addiction*
Mushrooms: *Psychedelic Fungi*
Nicotine: *An Old-Fashioned Addiction*
Over-The-Counter Drugs: *Harmless or Hazardous?*
PCP: *The Dangerous Angel*
Prescription Narcotics: *The Addictive Painkillers*
Quaaludes: *The Quest for Oblivion*
Teenage Depression and Drugs
Treating Mental Illness
Valium: *and Other Tranquilizers*

SERIES 2

Bad Trips
Brain Function
Case Histories
Celebrity Drug Use
Designer Drugs
The Downside of Drugs
Drinking, Driving, and Drugs
Drugs and Civilization
Drugs and Crime
Drugs and Diet
Drugs and Disease
Drugs and Emotion
Drugs and Pain
Drugs and Perception
Drugs and Pregnancy
Drugs and Sexual Behavior

Drugs and Sleep
Drugs and Sports
Drugs and the Arts
Drugs and the Brain
Drugs and the Family
Drugs and the Law
Drugs and Women
Drugs of the Future
Drugs Through the Ages
Drug Use Around the World
Legalization: *A Debate*
Mental Disturbances
Nutrition and the Brain
The Origins and Sources of Drugs
Substance Abuse: *Prevention and Treatment*
Who Uses Drugs?

MARIJUANA

THE ENCYCLOPEDIA OF PSYCHOACTIVE DRUGS

MARIJUANA

Its Effects on Mind & Body

WILLIAM J. HERMES
ANNE GALPERIN

CHELSEA HOUSE PUBLISHERS
NEW YORK   PHILADELPHIA

Chelsea House Publishers

EDITOR-IN-CHIEF: Remmel Nunn
MANAGING EDITOR: Karyn Gullen Browne
COPY CHIEF: Mark Rifkin
PICTURE EDITOR: Adrian G. Allen
ART DIRECTOR: Maria Epes
MANUFACTURING DIRECTOR: Gerald Levine
SYSTEMS MANAGER: Lindsey Ottman
PRODUCTION MANAGER: Joseph Romano

STAFF FOR MARIJUANA: ITS EFFECTS ON MIND & BODY
EDITOR: Brian Feinberg
SENIOR COPY EDITOR: Laurie Kahn
PRODUCTION EDITOR: Marie Claire Cebrián
CAPTIONS: Ann Keene
LAYOUT: Bernard Schleifer
APPENDIXES AND TABLES: Gary Tong
PICTURE RESEARCH: Wendy P. Wills

Library of Congress Cataloging-in-Publication Data
Galperin, Anne.
  Marijuana: its effects on mind and body/Anne Galperin and William J. Hermes.
  p. cm.—(Encyclopedia of psychoactive drugs)
  Includes index.
  Summary: Discusses the scientific, social, and personal aspects of marijuana,
examining its history, cultural impact, psychological and physical effects, dangers,
and legal status.
  ISBN 0-87754-754-8
     0-7910-0765-0 (pbk.)
  1. Marihuana—United States—Juvenile literature. 2. Marihuana—
Physiological effect—Juvenile literature. [1. Marihuana.] I. Hermes, William J.
II. Title. III. Series.
HV5809.5.G35   1992   91-17766
615'.7827—dc20   CIP
9 8 7 6 5 4 3   AC

CONTENTS

A young girl in Lebanon harvests cannabis plants as a first step in the production of hashish, a puttylike substance that is smoked in pipes or eaten. Hashish is a major source of income for thousands of Lebanese farmers; most of it is smuggled abroad.

FOREWORD

$\mathbf{S}$ince the 1960s, the abuse of psychoactive substances—drugs that alter mood and behavior—has grown alarmingly. Many experts in the fields of medicine, public health, law enforcement, and crime prevention are calling the situation an epidemic. Some legal psychoactive substances—alcohol, caffeine, and nicotine, for example—have been in use since colonial times; illegal ones such as heroin and marijuana have been used to a varying extent by certain segments of the population for decades. But only in the late 20th century has there been widespread reliance on such a variety of mind-altering substances—by youth as well as by adults.

Day after day, newspapers, magazines, and television and radio programs bring us the grim consequences of this dependence. Addiction threatens not only personal health but the stability of our communities and currently costs society an estimated $180 billion annually in the United States alone. Drug-related violent crime and death are increasingly becoming a way of life in many of our cities, towns, and rural areas alike.

Why do people use drugs of any kind? There is one simple answer: to "feel better," physically or mentally. The antibiotics your doctor prescribes for an ear infection destroy the bacteria and make the pain go away. Aspirin can make us more comfortable by reducing fever, banishing a headache, or relieving joint pain from arthritis. Cigarettes put smokers at ease in social situations; a beer or a cocktail helps a worker relax after a hard day on the job. Caffeine, the most widely

9

used drug in America, wakes us up in the morning and overcomes fatigue when we have exams to study for or a long drive to make. Prescription drugs, over-the-counter remedies, tobacco products, alcoholic beverages, caffeine products—all of these are legally available substances that have the capacity to change the way we feel.

But the drugs causing the most concern today are not found in a package of NoDoz or in an aspirin bottle. The drugs that government and private agencies are spending billions of dollars to overcome in the name of crime prevention, law enforcement, rehabilitation, and education have names like crack, angel dust, pot, horse, and speed. Cocaine, PCP, marijuana, heroin, and amphetamines can be very dangerous indeed, to both users and those with whom they live, go to school, and work. But other mood- and mind-altering substances are having a devastating impact, too—especially on youth.

Consider alcohol: The minimum legal drinking age in all 50 states is now 21, but adolescent consumption remains high, even as a decline in other forms of drug use is reported. A recent survey of high school seniors reveals that on any given weekend one in three seniors will be drunk; more than half of all high school seniors report that they have driven while they were drunk. The average age at which a child has his or her first drink is now 12, and more than 1 in 3 eighth-graders report having been drunk at least once.

Or consider nicotine, the psychoactive and addictive ingredient of tobacco: While smoking has declined in the population as a whole, the number of adolescent girls who smoke has been steadily increasing. Because certain health hazards of smoking have been conclusively demonstrated—its relationship to heart disease, lung cancer, and respiratory disease; its link to premature birth and low birth weight of babies whose mothers smoked during pregnancy—the long-term effects of such a trend are a cause for concern.

Studies have shown that almost all drug abuse begins in the preteen and teenage years. It is not difficult to understand why: Adolescence is a time of tremendous change and turmoil, when teenagers face the tasks of discovering their identity, clarifying their sexual roles, asserting their independence as they learn to cope with authority, and searching for goals. The pressures—from friends, parents, teachers, coaches, and one's own self—are great, and the temptation to want to "feel better" by taking drugs is powerful.

Psychoactive drugs are everywhere in our society, and their use and misuse show no sign of waning. The lack of success in the so-called war on drugs, begun in earnest in the 1980s, has shown us that we cannot "drug proof" our homes, schools, workplaces, and communities. What we can do, however, is make available the latest information on these substances and their effects and ask that those reading it consider the information carefully.

The newly updated ENCYCLOPEDIA OF PSYCHOACTIVE DRUGS, specifically written for young people, provides up-to-date information on a variety of substances that are widely abused in today's society. Each volume is devoted to a specific substance or pattern of abuse and is designed to answer the questions that young readers are likely to ask about drugs. An individualized glossary in each volume defines key words and terms, and newly enlarged and updated appendixes include recent statistical data as well as a special section on AIDS and its relation to drug abuse. The editors of the ENCYCLOPEDIA OF PSYCHOACTIVE DRUGS hope this series will help today's adolescents make intelligent choices as they prepare for maturity in the 21st century.

Ann Keene, Editor

A section of leaves from a wild marijuana plant. Although a 1982 report stated that there is no proof that marijuana causes birth defects, recent evidence suggests that use of the drug may affect the body's genetic material.

USES AND ABUSES

Jack H. Mendelson, M.D.
Nancy K. Mello, Ph.D.
Alcohol and Drug Abuse Research Center
Harvard Medical School—McLean Hospital

*H*uman beings are endowed with the gift of wizardry, a talent for discovery and invention. The discovery and invention of substances that change the way we feel and behave are among our special accomplishments, and like so many other products of our wizardry, these substances have the capacity to harm as well as to help.

Consider alcohol—available to all and recognized as both harmful and pleasure inducing since biblical times. The use of alcoholic beverages dates back to our earliest ancestors. Alcohol use and misuse became associated with the worship of gods and demons. One of the most powerful Greek gods was Dionysus, lord of fruitfulness and god of wine. The Romans adopted Dionysus but changed his name to Bacchus. Festivals and holidays associated with Bacchus celebrated the harvest and the origins of life. Time has blurred the images of the Bacchanalian festival, but the theme of drunkenness as a major part of celebration has survived the pagan gods and remains a familiar part of modern society. The term *Bacchanalian festival* conveys a more appealing image than "drunken orgy" or "pot party," but whatever the label, some of the celebrants will inevitably start up the "high" escalator to the next plateau. Once there, the de-escalation is often difficult.

According to reliable estimates, 1 out of every 10 Americans develops a serious alcohol-related problem sometime in his or her lifetime. In addition, automobile accidents caused by drunken drivers claim the lives of more than 20,000 people each year, and injure 25 times that number. Many of the victims are gifted young people just starting out in adult life. Hospital emergency rooms abound with patients seeking help for alcohol-related injuries.

Who is to blame? Can we blame the many manufacturers who produce such an amazing variety of alcoholic beverages? Should we blame the educators who fail to explain the perils of intoxication or so exaggerate the dangers of drinking that no one could possibly believe them? Are friends to blame— those peers who urge others to "drink more and faster," or the macho types who stress the importance of being able to "hold your liquor?" Casting blame, however, is hardly constructive, and pointing the finger is a fruitless way to deal with problems. Alcoholism and drug abuse have few culprits but many victims. Accountability begins with each of us, every time we choose to use or to misuse an intoxicating substance.

It is ironic that some of our earliest medicines, derived from natural plant products, are used today to poison and to intoxicate. Relief from pain and suffering is one of society's many continuing goals. More than 3,000 years ago, the Therapeutic Papyrus of Thebes, one of our earliest written records, gave instructions for the use of opium in the treatment of pain. Opium, in the form of its major derivative, morphine, remains one of the most powerful drugs we have for pain relief. But opium, morphine, and similar compounds, such as heroin, have also been used by many to induce changes in mood and feeling. Another example of a natural substance that has been misused is the coca leaf, which for centuries was used by the Indians of Peru to reduce fatigue and hunger. Its modern derivative, cocaine, has important medical use as a local anesthetic. Unfortunately, its increasing abuse in recent years has reached epidemic proportions.

The purpose of this series is to provide information about the nature and behavioral effects of alcohol and drugs and the probable consequences of their use. The authors believe that up-to-date, objective information about alcohol and drugs will help readers make better decisions about the wisdom of their use. The information presented here (and in other books in this series) is based on many clinical and laboratory studies and observations by people from diverse walks of life.

Over the centuries, novelists, poets, and dramatists have provided us with many insights into the effects of alcohol and drug use. Physicians, lawyers, biologists, psychologists, and social scientists have contributed to a better understanding of the causes and consequences of using these substances. The authors in this series have attempted to gather and condense all the latest information about drug use. They have also described the sometimes wide gaps in our knowledge and have suggested some new ways to answer many difficult questions.

How, for example, do alcohol and drug problems get started? And what is the best way to treat them when they do? Not too many years ago, alcoholics and drug abusers were regarded as evil, immoral, or both. Many now believe that these persons suffer from very complicated diseases involving deep psychological and social problems. To understand how the disease begins and progresses, it is necessary to understand the nature of the substance, the behavior of the afflicted person, and the characteristics of the society or culture in which that person lives.

The diagram below shows the interaction of these three factors. The arrows indicate that the substance not only affects the user personally but the society as well. Society influences attitudes toward the substance, which in turn affect its availability. The substance's impact upon the society may support or discourage the use and abuse of that substance.

SUBSTANCE
(ALCOHOL OR DRUG)

PERSON ◄──────────► SOCIETY

Although many of the social environments we live in are very similar, some of the most subtle differences can strongly influence our thinking and behavior. Where we live, go to school and work, whom we discuss things with—all influence our opinions about drug use. Yet we also share certain commonly accepted beliefs that outweigh any differences in our attitudes. The authors in this series have tried to identify and discuss the central, most crucial issues concerning drug use.

A U.S. Customs inspector uses insulated gloves to handle a still-smoldering brick of marijuana from a cache of 6,000 pounds found smuggled aboard a tanker truck in Miami. The marijuana caught fire when Customs workers used a blowtorch to get at the contraband. A drug-sniffing dog alerted officials to the truck as it was off-loaded from a Jamaican ship.

Regrettably, human wizardry in developing new substances in medical therapeutics has not always been paralleled by intelligent usage. Although we do know a great deal about the effects of alcohol and drugs, we have yet to learn how to impart that knowledge, especially to young adults.

Does it matter? What harm does it do to smoke a little pot or have a few beers? What is it like to be intoxicated? How long does it last? Will it make me feel really fine? Will it make me sick? What are the risks? These are but a few of the questions answered in this series, which we hope will enable the reader to make wise decisions concerning the crucial issue of drugs.

Information sensibly acted upon can go a long way toward helping everyone develop his or her best self. As one keen and sensitive observer, Dr. Lewis Thomas, has said,

> *There is nothing at all absurd about the human condition. We matter. It seems to me a good guess, hazarded by a good many people who have thought about it, that we may be engaged in the formation of something like a mind for the life of this planet. If this is so, we are still at the most primitive stage, still fumbling with language and thinking, but infinitely capacitated for the future. Looked at this way, it is remarkable that we've come as far as we have in so short a period, really no time at all as geologists measure time. We are the newest, the youngest, and the brightest thing around.*

Male (right) and female marijuana plants. The female plant produces flowers, called buds, which are more potent than leaves from either sex.

CHAPTER 1

MARIJUANA: AN OVERVIEW

*M*arijuana (also called weed, pot, herb, ganja, sensi, and innumerable other names) is the term generally used to describe the flowering tops and leaves of the *Indian hemp plant*. Its history as a mood-altering, or *psychoactive*, substance dates back hundreds of years; many cultures still use it for medicinal purposes, during meditation and religious worship, and as an intoxicant.

According to a 1988 government survey, marijuana is the third most widely used drug in the United States, after alcohol and cigarettes. It is the single most widely used illegal drug in the country. An estimated 66 million people—or one-third of all Americans—have tried marijuana; and roughly 12 million of them are current users. Among U.S. high school students, it is estimated that 44% have tried the drug and that 17% use it with some regularity. There seems to be no typical marijuana user, and its use is not limited to any one segment of society.

The Marijuana Plant

The Indian hemp plant (genus *Cannabis*) is a weed that grows freely throughout many parts of the world, including North America. It has been farmed for thousands of years as a source of fiber for making rope, cloth, and paper; as a source of food for humans, livestock, and birds (its seeds provide complete vegetable protein); as a source of seed oil for lamp fuel, lubrication, and oil-based paints; and more recently, for marijuana.

Richard Shultes, a Harvard-based botanist, has identified three distinct varieties, or strains, of the plant. *Cannabis sativa* is a loosely branched plant that can reach a height of 18 feet. *Cannabis indica* is a smaller, more densely branched plant, often cone-shaped, and usually no more than four feet in height. *Cannabis ruderalis* is a small, dense plant with few or no branches that grows to between one and three feet high and is indigenous to parts of Asia.

These strains are able to crossbreed freely, allowing hemp growers over the years to develop certain characteristics in their crop through selective breeding and advanced growing techniques. As a result, there are numerous other strains that do not fit neatly under any of the above headings. (Certain varieties grown in Italy for paper fiber, for instance, are reputed to reach 35 feet in height.)

More than 400 separate chemical compounds have been isolated in marijuana. Those that are unique to this particular plant are known as *cannabinoids*. *Delta-9 tetrahydrocannabinol* (THC) is the specific cannabinoid most responsible for producing the marijuana "high." Other cannabinoids, including *cannabidiol* (CBD) and *cannabinol* (CBN), may also contribute to marijuana's psychoactive properties; but more research is needed in this area.

The potency of marijuana is determined by the amount of THC it contains, and this can vary widely in different plants, ranging from 1% to more than 10%. The THC content in marijuana is dependent on many factors: the sex of the plant (female plants generally produce more potent marijuana than do males), the genetics of the plant, the soil and climate in which it is grown, and the parts of the plant used (flowers, commonly called *buds*, are more potent than leaves).

Whereas hemp plants were at one time bred in the United States and abroad to maximize their fiber content or seed count, growers are now more concerned with increasing the plant's THC content, so as to produce more potent marijuana that in turn will command higher prices. (The best grade of marijuana can sell for as much as $600 per ounce, according to *High Times* magazine, which covers the drug culture. The average THC content of available marijuana increased somewhat during the 1980s, according to some reports; this potent domestic marijuana, grown under exacting conditions, has apparently filled the market gap left by the less potent imports being stopped at the borders.

Marijuana Cultivation Cannabis is a hardy, tenacious annual plant that thrives under a variety of environmental conditions. In the United States, reports show that cannabis is not only cultivated but also grows wild in virtually every state. Most domestic marijuana, however, comes from Hawaii, northern California, Oregon, Kentucky, and other states with the damp, temperate climate well suited for raising the plant. Marijuana can also be grown indoors, a method that has become popular among some growers in the interest of avoiding detection. A small industry has grown up around indoor cultivation, with a proliferation of how-to books and growing supplies marketed for the more or less obvious purpose of growing cannabis plants.

So-called Thai sticks were popularized in the United States in the late 1960s by soldiers returning from the Vietnam War. The sticks, made from a very potent marijuana called sinsemilla, have a THC content of 6% or more.

The life cycle of various strains of cannabis plants can vary greatly. Generally speaking, however, the cycle runs from four to nine months. It takes from 3 to 10 days for the plant to sprout, and the seedling (young plant) stage is completed after 4 to 6 weeks. Flowering usually lasts one to two months, with males flowering a few weeks before females. The female plant will produce fruit (seeds) in two to five weeks following pollination, when the pollen of the male flower is brought into contact with the female flower, usually via the wind.

Sinsemilla An increasingly popular form of marijuana is called *sinsemilla*, which means "without seeds." To grow sinsemilla, the female cannabis plant must be prevented from being fertilized by the pollen of the male plant, so that its flowering buds will not produce seeds. Marijuana seeds contain only traces of THC, and because the drug is usually sold by weight, users prefer to buy sinsemilla.

Sinsemilla also has a reputation for being the most potent form of marijuana, but even though the flowering female buds generally contain more THC than other parts of the plant, seedless buds are not necessarily stronger than those with seeds. However, because sinsemilla is usually grown under carefully controlled conditions, it is likely to be particularly potent.

Other Drugs Derived from Cannabis

Hashish (or *hash*) is a preparation traditionally made by thrashing cannabis plants over a screen and compacting the resinous material that collects into a puttylike mass. This form of the drug is common throughout India, parts of the Middle East, and northern Africa; most hashish in the United States is smuggled into the country from these areas. Like other types of marijuana, hashish varies widely in potency, its THC content ranging from 1% to more than 12%. It can be smoked in pipes or eaten.

Hash oil is a highly concentrated extract of resinous oil from cannabis flowers and may contain between 1% and 60% THC. THC is very unstable in oil form and is subject to rapid deterioration from exposure to air and light; hence, hash oil potency varies greatly.

Methods of Marijuana Use

Smoking Although it can be eaten in food or made into a tea, marijuana is most commonly smoked. In addition to being a social ritual among users, smoking is also the quickest way to get THC into the bloodstream. Users draw marijuana smoke deep into their lungs from either a pipe or cigarette (often referred to as a *joint* or *spliff*) and hold it there for several seconds in order to maximize the drug's effect.

Like most drugs, marijuana affects different people in different ways. Many first-time users experience nothing at all, others feel a sense of profound relaxation, and still others may experience feelings of agitation and alienation. Many find that marijuana makes them talkative and more social, whereas some users tend to become quiet and introspective. In ad-

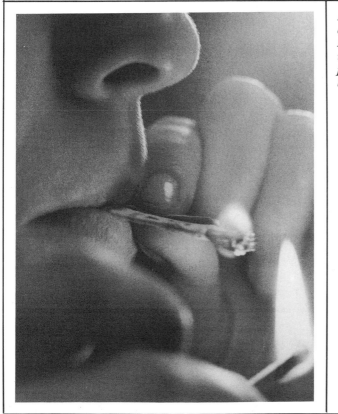

A youthful pot smoker draws on a joint. Marijuana is usually rolled in cigarette paper and smoked like tobacco.

dition, some people even believe the drug heightens their creativity and improves their ability to concentrate, while others find themselves unable to follow a simple train of thought. Many users have experienced each of these sensations on occasion. The variability of marijuana's effect appears to be the result of a combination of factors, including the strength of the sample and an individual's mood before getting high.

When smoked, the effects of marijuana generally come in two stages. The initial phase occurs within a few minutes of smoking and can last anywhere between 30 minutes and an hour. It is usually characterized by a jumbled rush of ideas; in addition, the perception of sound, color, scent, taste, and touch seem intensified. These sensations may come in waves and are often accompanied by an increase in heart rate. The second phase is usually one of repose and sleepiness, which can last from two to three hours or longer.

Eating The effects of eating marijuana are similar to those of smoking it, except that a larger amount is needed to obtain the same high, the onset of the drug's effects is slower, and the period of intoxication lasts longer. Marijuana is commonly baked into cookies or brownies or cooked into stews or sauces in order to mask its vaguely unpleasant taste.

Because it is even more difficult to estimate dosage when eating marijuana than when smoking it, there is a greater chance of ingesting too much of the drug. Excessive amounts of marijuana may cause episodes of extreme anxiety and confusion, usually followed by an extended period of sleep.

Health Issues

It is hard to determine the full spectrum of health risks associated with marijuana use. As an intoxicant, the drug distorts perception of time and distance and can impair a person's ability to drive an automobile or operate machinery. A number of studies have shown that marijuana can damage short-term memory (see Chapter 5), although it is unclear whether memory improves once marijuana use stops. The drug has also been implicated as a contributing factor in a wide range of psychological and personality problems, including lack of motivation, decreased attention span, and feelings of isolation.

In addition, there have been studies connecting marijuana smoking to lesions in the lungs that may, eventually, turn cancerous, as well as to impairment of the immune system (which fights infection and disease) and the reproductive system. Because of the shortage of conclusive research, however, the dangers of long-term use remain uncertain.

On the other hand, some health disorders have been found to respond favorably to treatment with marijuana. The drug has been used to combat the nausea and loss of appetite that accompany treatment for both cancer and acquired immune deficiency syndrome (AIDS). Marijuana has also been found to reduce damaging pressure within the eye caused by glaucoma, and reports indicate that the drug may ease breathing during asthma attacks. Because of the drug's illegal status, however, it continues to be banned from use as a medication except in an exceedingly small number of cases. This will be more fully discussed in Chapter 7.

An assortment of paraphernalia from the early 1980s used to smoke marijuana

Addiction The question of whether users become physically addicted to marijuana is unclear, but research indicates that some may develop a tolerance—that is, they may need to keep increasing the amount they use in order to get the desired effect. (There have also have been reports of sleeplessness, appetite loss, and increased anxiety when heavy smokers abruptly stop using it). To the extent that users enjoy marijuana and seek to repeat their experiences, it is considered *psychologically addictive*. That is, the mind grows dependent on the drug, so much so, in fact, that users may spend a large part of the day thinking about their next joint or planning where they can buy more marijuana. What constitutes abuse of the drug, though, is not clearly or uniformly defined. Some consider any use of an illegal substance to be abuse, while others draw the line once the user's health, work performance, or interpersonal relationships begin to deteriorate. Treatment to help people stop using marijuana usually takes the form of programs similar to treatment techniques used by Alcoholics Anonymous.

Gateway to Danger?

Many refer to marijuana as a *gateway drug*, meaning that those who use it sometimes go on to try stronger substances in pursuit of a greater "high." Although many individuals who use harder drugs such as cocaine and heroin also use marijuana, the existence of an inevitable link from marijuana to harder substances has not been proved.

Legal Issues

Marijuana use in the United States was effectively banned by federal law in 1937, ostensibly for reasons of public health. Today, however, much of the opposition to marijuana is linked to political and moral considerations. Everywhere in the United States, the drug remains illegal to possess, grow, or sell. In some states, though, including California, Colorado, Maine, Minnesota, Mississippi, Nevada, New York, North Carolina, Ohio, and Oregon, marijuana offenses have, to an extent, been *decriminalized*. Decriminalization of marijuana does not mean that it becomes legal, just that possession of a small amount—usually less than one ounce—is no longer considered a criminal offense. Instead, it becomes what is known as a civil offense, like a parking violation, and the penalties are either eliminated, or downgraded from jail time to a fine.

It has commonly been assumed that criminal penalties for the possession of marijuana deter people from using the drug. This has clearly not proved to be the case. In addition, it has been assumed that marijuana decriminalization or legalization would lead to a substantial increase in use. In states where marijuana has been decriminalized, however, its use is reported to be no more prevalent than in areas that have stricter penalties.

As an illegal drug, marijuana is part of the complicated matrix of our national drug problem. Yet some people believe that marijuana, because of its comparatively mild nature, should be considered separately from drugs such as crack (the potent, smokable derivative of cocaine that first came onto the scene in the mid-1980s) and heroin. The meteoric rise of crack use in the United States during the mid- to late 1980s, however, largely sidelined the debates over marijuana use and decriminalization that had garnered media attention during the previous two decades.

Following a raid by his officers, a sheriff stands amid a bumper crop of marijuana plants under cultivation at a farm near Calhoun, Georgia, in the early 1980s. The crop's street value was then estimated at $1.5 million.

Marijuana (Cannabis sativa) *leaves, flowers, and seeds, as illustrated in* **Medicinal Plants,** *published in 1880. In 1894 the* Encyclopedia Britannica *estimated that 300 million people were using the drug.*

CHAPTER 2

MARIJUANA IN HISTORY

Cannabis is one of the oldest known agricultural plants. As a result, its presence in the history of world culture is extensive. Archaeologists believe that the earliest woven fabrics may have been made from hemp fibers between 8000 and 7000 B.C.

Hemp Use in China

The first solid evidence of hemp use, however, comes from the Yang-shao culture of China (about 4500 B.C.), which is thought to have used the plant fibers initially for rope and net making and later in the development of cloth weaving. Hemp fibers are separated from the stem of the cannabis plant when the stem rots, a process known as *retting*.

Ancient Chinese cultures used the cannabis plant for other purposes as well. There is evidence that hemp seed was an important food source in China from prehistoric times until the 6th century A.D., when it was displaced by more palatable grains. Paper made of hemp fiber dating back to approximately 100 B.C. was unearthed recently in graves in Shaanxi province; these are the oldest paper samples yet found.

The use of the flowering tops and leaves of the cannabis plant—what we now know as marijuana—was also first recorded by the Chinese. The *Pên-ts'ao Ching,* the world's earliest pharmacopeia (presumed to have been written originally by Emperor Shen-Nung around 2800 B.C.) notes the psychoactive properties of the drug, along with its usefulness in treating a variety of medical disorders, including rheumatism and menstrual pains, gout, constipation, and forgetfulness.

India and Other Parts of the World

The Aryan, or Indo-Persian, culture of India documented the use of marijuana—known as *bhang*—in a group of religious books known as the four *Vedas*, which were compiled between 1400 and 1000 B.C. In the fourth book, the *Atharvaveda*, marijuana is referred to as one of the "five kingdoms of herbs ... which release us from anxiety." In the Aryan

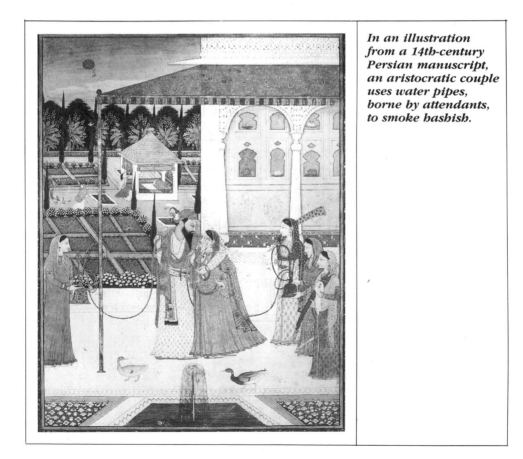

In an illustration from a 14th-century Persian manuscript, an aristocratic couple uses water pipes, borne by attendants, to smoke hashish.

tradition, marijuana was considered a sacred substance, and it played an important role in religious rituals. Marijuana use became common because of its association with religious practices. It was commonly used in the Sufi religious order and played a central role in Tibetan tantric tradition.

Archaeologists assume that the cannabis plant was introduced to the Middle East and Europe via the Aryans and other nomadic tribes. In the 5th century A.D., the Greek historian Herodotus wrote about the practices of the nomadic Scythian people, who inhaled the smoke of burning cannabis during funeral ceremonies. There is evidence that cannabis was cultivated in Norway as far back as 400 B.C. and in England and Germany by A.D. 400.

Cannabis in America

Over the centuries, cannabis cultivation spread throughout Asia, Africa, and Europe. Although some believe that marijuana was known to Native Americans before Columbus, cannabis was probably introduced to the Americas by the Spaniards, who brought cannabis seeds to Chile around 1545.

In North America, the plant was first grown in Virginia in 1611 and in Massachussetts in the 1630s. Britain, a strong naval power, had come to depend on hemp fiber for the ropes and sails of its fleets. This dependence made cannabis into an important cash crop and one so essential that early colonial law actually mandated that farmers grow the plant. (The name for the material employed in sail making—canvas—is in fact derived from the word *cannabis*.) So central was cannabis to the economy of the colonies that people could actually use it to pay their taxes: It was considered legal tender from 1631 to the beginning of the 19th century. Both George Washington and Thomas Jefferson grew cannabis on their plantations.

An Essential Crop A large-scale U.S. hemp industry had begun in Kentucky by 1776, and by 1860 it was almost as important as the South's cotton industry. By 1890, however, domestic hemp production went into decline; labor-saving machinery gave the cotton industry a boost, whereas hemp harvesting still required a great deal of manual labor. The Civil War further disrupted the hemp industry, and in subsequent years the combination of foreign fiber imports and

Visitors to the Turkish booth at an 1876 centennial exposition, sample the novelty of smoking hashish from a water pipe. Hemp, the source of marijuana and hashish, was grown in the United States to make rope and sailcloth as early as 1611, but recreational use in the United States was not reported until 1910.

the continued lack of efficient harvesting methods prevented its recovery.

Medicinal Use There is little evidence that marijuana was used recreationally in the United States during the 17th and 18th centuries. However, following a series of enthusiastic reports by researchers, it became popular as a medicine in the mid-19th century. More than 100 articles discussing marijuana's value in treating ailments such as headaches, insomnia, and menstrual cramps were published in North American medical journals between 1840 and 1900. Pharmaceutical companies marketed marijuana in a wide variety of preparations, and it was available in most drugstores through the beginning of the 20th century.

A Recreational Drug Use of marijuana for its intoxicating effects was first noted in the United States during the late 19th and early 20th centuries. Mexican and Caribbean immigrant laborers introduced the practice of smoking marijuana to the southern and southwestern parts of the country—especially Texas, Louisiana, and New Mexico. Meanwhile, hashish smoking became popular among select groups in eastern cities such as New York and Chicago after Turkish merchants introduced the substance at international expositions. By the 1880s, the *Police Gazette* estimated that there were more than 500 hashish parlors operating in New York City alone.

During this period, marijuana use was also popularized through the arts. In 1857, Fitz Hugh Ludlow, a close friend and contemporary of Mark Twain, published *The Hasheesh Eater*, which described his personal experiments with the drug. In addition, marijuana use became popular among some New Orleans jazz musicians in the early 20th century; and later, recordings such as "Reefer Song" by Fats Waller, "Texas Tea Party" by Benny Goodman, and "Muggles" by Louis Armstrong referred—often humorously—to the drug.

Public Concern over Marijuana Around the beginning of the 20th century, public concern began to grow around the issue of marijuana smoking, largely in response to sensational tales of its supposed dangers. Magazines and newspapers printed headlines about the "marijuana menace," with stories that attributed gory murders to the use of "killer weed."

Most of these stories, however, were greatly exaggerated; they were inspired mainly by racist sentiment toward blacks and Mexicans, who commonly used the drug. As the economic pressures that culminated in the depression escalated, negative attitudes grew with regard to immigrant groups, who were often blamed for the nation's fiscal woes. Conflicts grew between immigrant and native populations, especially in border towns such as El Paso. Prohibiting marijuana use, which was a part of immigrant culture, was an easy way to justify harassment of newcomers. Between 1914 and 1931, 29 states—mostly those with high immigrant populations—passed laws that made it a criminal offense to possess or use marijuana.

Use of the drug by members of the military also became a concern during this period. U.S. soldiers stationed in the area formerly known as the Panama Canal Zone were reported to be smoking marijuana regularly. In response, bejtween 1916 and 1929 the army conducted an investigation into the effects of the drug; the report concluded that moderate use of marijuana was neither habit forming nor dangerous.

The marijuana "problem" remained a state and local issue through most of the 1930s, as alcohol prohibition (1920–33) and narcotics abuse occupied attention on a national level. (Narcotics are drugs that depress the central nervous system and are used medically to alleviate pain. Marijuana does not fall into this category.) Moreover, the federal government was unsure whether it was even constitutionally possible to outlaw marijuana, as such a step would in effect constitute a regulation of both domestic hemp production and the medical profession.

Federal Regulation of Marijuana

The late 1930s, however, marked a turning point for cannabis in the United States. On the one hand, the plant's viability as a commercial fiber crop was revived because of the development of the *hemp decorticator*, a machine that could efficiently process cut cannabis both for paper-making material and fabric fiber. A 1938 *Popular Mechanics* article proclaimed cannabis the "New Billion Dollar Crop" and foresaw veritable revolutions in both the textile and paper industries as domestically grown hemp displaced imported fibers and supplanted wood pulp for making paper products.

The Marijuana Tax Act On the other hand, antipathy toward marijuana use was reaching a crescendo. By 1937, all but two states had enacted their own antimarijuana laws. Regional politicians and law enforcement agencies, along with Harry J. Anslinger, director of the newly established Federal Bureau of Narcotics (now the Drug Enforcement Administration), were pushing for national marijuana legislation. Finally, the Treasury Department drew up the Marijuana Tax Act, which required all manufacturers, importers, wholesale dealers, pharmacists, and medical practitioners handling the substance to pay a variety of occupational and

A 1942 photograph shows a spinning-machine operator in the South converting hemp fiber into loose strands that will be made into rope. The production of hemp, a major farm crop in the United States for more than 100 years, declined in the early 20th century but was revived briefly during World War II.

transactional taxes for dealing with marijuana. The tax effectively outlawed the substance for recreational use by requiring written order forms for all transactions and by establishing a large tax on the transfer of marijuana to unregistered persons.

A number of interest groups, including the American Medical Association and various representatives of the hemp and pharmaceutical industries, petitioned unsuccessfully against the bill's passage. It appeared to many that cannabis was being outlawed less for its harmful effects, which had not been proven, than for an excuse to harass the immigrant and minority groups who commonly smoked it. Some believe that certain corporate interests, threatened by the renewed viability of commercial cannabis, also helped push the bill through. Whatever the reasons, the act was quietly passed by Congress in September of 1937 with little substantive debate.

The Tax Act hastened marijuana's disappearance as an ingredient in patent medicines, and the drug was dropped from the *United States Pharmacopeia* (a book providing an extensive list of medicines) in 1941. The bill also prevented the resurgence of the hemp industry, although farmers were later encouraged to grow cannabis when the Japanese cut off U.S. sources of imported fiber during World War II. (A film documenting this campaign, entitled *Hemp for Victory*, was made by the U.S. Department of Agriculture in 1942.)

Harsh Penalties During the 1940s and 1950s, however, attitudes toward marijuana use remained negative. Popular belief held that marijuana use incited violence and was inevitably a stepping-stone to heroin addiction. Moreover, a purported rise in heroin and cocaine use led to the passage in 1951 of the Boggs Act, which established mandatory penalties of two to five years in prison and stiff fines for violation of any national drug laws, including the Marijuana Tax Act. The Narcotic Control Act of 1956 further toughened these laws. It was thought that harsher penalties would eliminate the drug problem, but this did not prove to be the case.

The Resurgence of Marijuana Use in the 1960s

In the mid-1960s the government again increased existing penalties for possession and use of marijuana, a change that coincided with the emergence of the so-called counterculture movement of the same period. Along with a political agenda that included ending the war in Vietnam, readdressing civil rights issues, and challenging environmental abuses, many involved in this movement were championing the use of marijuana, along with hallucinogens such as LSD, as a way to enhance experience and "free the mind." In addition, marijuana use became common among the many U.S. servicemen stationed abroad in Southeast Asia, some of whom continued the practice upon their return home.

During this period of escalated use, marijuana's status as a narcotic—a title it acquired from legislation rather than from any similarity to opiate narcotics—was disputed. By observation and experience, many people concluded that marijuana was a benign substance. In addition to casting suspicion on the entire antidrug consensus, stringent laws

Students at a 1960s gathering use a homemade pipe to smoke marijuana. Similar "smoke-ins" were a frequent occurrence in the counterculture of the 1960s and 1970s.

against marijuana served to fan the fires of antiauthority sentiment. Use of marijuana quickly evolved into a political symbol, a challenge to what was perceived as an unreasonable status quo. Widespread use of marijuana, public misconceptions regarding it, and laws that jailed citizens for possession of a single marijuana cigarette made marijuana an issue of considerable debate, one that demanded some sort of solution.

Addressing the Marijuana Question

In 1974, however, the federal government established the National Institute on Drug Abuse (NIDA) in order to solve the nation's drug abuse problem via research and public education. (Previously there had been only piecemeal studies performed on the physical and sociological effects of marijuana.)

During the 1970s and early 1980s, NIDA and other organizations sponsored numerous studies on marijuana, but this flurry of research seemed to raise more questions about the substance than it answered. Marijuana was shown to be a fairly complex drug; although some concerns about its effects were found to be exaggerated, neither was it shown to be completely harmless (see Chapter 5). In the mid- to late 1980s, however, research shifted away from marijuana and focused instead on cocaine and crack use because of the clear and devastating societal effects of the latter two drugs.

The Fight for Change Concern over the severity of punishment dealt to marijuana users led to the formation of the National Organization for the Reform of Marijuana Laws (NORML) in 1970. This organization continues to lobby actively toward decriminalization of the drug, recognition of its legitimate medical uses, and further research into its effects.

Efforts also began on numerous other fronts to reduce the penalties for personal use of marijuana. In 1972, the National Commission on Marihuana and Drug Abuse issued a report entitled *Marihuana: Signal of Misunderstanding* that recommended its decriminalization. (Marihuana is an alternate spelling of the word.) President Jimmy Carter came out in support of decriminalizing the possession of small amounts of marijuana (less than an ounce) during an address to Congress on the drug abuse problem in 1977.

Reduced Penalties As a result of initiatives against harsh marijuana penalties, many states amended their pot laws during the 1970s. Alaska made it permissible to possess the drug for personal consumption in one's own home under the constitutional right to privacy. (This stand was reversed in 1990, although as of early 1991 it was still uncertain whether the reversal would remain in effect.) As mentioned in Chapter 1, 10 other states decriminalized marijuana so that generally, the penalty for possession of a small amount of the drug was simply a fine (usually less than $200) issued like a traffic ticket.

Attitudes toward marijuana use began to shift in the 1980s. In the wake of the nation's "war on drugs," tolerance toward marijuana waned. Surveys indicated that use of the drug was in decline, and some states that had liberalized marijuana laws in the 1970s began talk of increasing penalties again. Overall, debate around marijuana receded from the national limelight during this period, but its use among certain segments of the population persisted.

Devices for marijuana users—a cigarette-rolling machine and a set of pipes—are offered for sale along with tourist souvenirs in the window of a New York City novelty shop in 1975. Despite the illegality of marijuana, merchandise related to its use continues to be openly bought and sold in some areas of the United States.

Holding a machete and several marijuana plants, Governor Henry Bellmon walks down a highway near Hinton, Oklahoma, in August 1989, inspecting the destruction of more than 180,000 marijuana plants by state highway patrolmen and sheriff's deputies.

CHAPTER 3

MARIJUANA AND THE LAW

In the United States, the possession, sale, and cultivation of marijuana are prohibited by federal law. Though some may find the laws too moderate and others may believe they are too harsh, an estimated 12 million or more Americans still use marijuana at least once a month. In 1989, according to a December 1990 article in the *Philadelphia Inquirer*, more than 314,000 persons were arrested for marijuana possession in the United States: These represented one-third of all drug arrests made in the country. During 1979, at the peak of the nation's marijuana use, 391,600 people were arrested for possession.

The Comprehensive Drug Abuse Prevention and Control Act of 1970 downgraded marijuana possession from a felony to a misdemeanor. However, the Controlled Substances Act of 1970 established it as a *Schedule I* drug—an illicit substance with a high potential for abuse and no known medical value—along with heroin and LSD. The sale of marijuana was now punishable by up to 15 years in prison and a $25,000 fine. Penalties for possession of small amounts of marijuana currently vary from state to state and can include a fine or imprisonment or both.

Law Enforcement

Since 1973, the Drug Enforcement Administration (DEA) has been the federal agency mandated to enforce narcotics and controlled substances law. The DEA carries out its mandate to stop the marijuana trade in many ways.

Foreign Eradication Efforts The DEA's efforts include targeting cannabis grown in foreign countries, provided that their governments are cooperative. In late 1976, the U.S. and Mexican governments worked together to spray a potent herbicide, *paraquat*, on marijuana fields in Mexico. This was done despite evidence that the substance is toxic to humans and can damage the lungs, heart, kidneys, muscles, and brain. This presented a danger to pot smokers when farmers, attempting to save their crop, harvested the marijuana just after it was sprayed. During late 1976 and early 1977, 21% of Mexican-grown marijuana intercepted at the U.S. border was contaminated with paraquat. Not all of the tainted imports were caught, however, and many people in the United States unwittingly smoked paraquat-treated marijuana. (A 1983 *Newsweek* article stated that although no cases of lung poisoning had been traced to marijuana tainted with the herbicide, U.S. health officials estimated that many thousands of pot users had inhaled enough paraquat to pose a health risk.) As people learned more about crop contamination, many individuals turned to domestically grown marijuana. Paraquat has also been used for crop eradication in the United States: According to the DEA, the federal government last used it to destroy marijuana in Kentucky and Georgia during the early 1980s.

Current Domestic Eradication Efforts It is now estimated that anywhere from one-quarter to one-half of the marijuana smoked in the United States is domestically produced. Based on federal figures, NORML calculated the retail cash value of the 1988 domestic marijuana/hemp crop at $41 billion, making it the country's leading cash crop.

The DEA's Domestic Cannabis Eradication/Suppression Program (DCE/SP) spent $3.8 million annually between 1987 and 1989. The DCE/SP is a coordinated effort among federal, state, and local agencies. Those involved include law enforcement officers, special agents, rangers, and others from the U.S. Forest Service, the Bureau of Land Management, the Fish and Wildlife Service, the National Park Service, the Bureau of Indian Affairs, the U.S. Air Force, the Civil Air Patrol, and the National Guard.

According to the DCE/SP's report on 1989 eradication activities:

•The DEA destroyed almost 130 million cannabis plants in the United States, which weighed more than 2,750 tons altogether: More than 124 million of these plants were *ditchweed* (low-potency, wild-growing cannabis); the remainder, more than 5 million specimens, were cultivated plants, 2 million of which were identified as sinsemilla. This represents an increase over the 107 million domestic plants destroyed by the DEA in 1988.

•The United States became the world's second leading producer of marijuana (the first being Mexico) as a result of a 65% drop in Colombian marijuana cultivation between 1988 and 1989. The DEA reports that what may actually be occurring in Colombia is a shift from growing marijuana to cultivating coca, from which cocaine is made, because the latter brings more money to farmers.

•About $29.5 million in assets (such as cars, boats, computers, and cash) were taken from marijuana growers, a dramatic increase over the $9.8 million taken in 1988. The strict *zero-*

(continued on page 46)

Harry J. Anslinger (left), director of the newly established Federal Bureau of Narcotics, watches as agents of the FBN prepare to burn packages of marijuana seized in a raid in the fall of 1937.

THE MARIJUANA INDUSTRY

By 1988, NORML estimated marijuana to be America's number one cash crop, calculating the value of that year's harvest at a staggering $41 billion. The U.S. corn crop for the same year was valued at about $13.4 billion; soybeans at $11.9 billion.

According to government surveys, although marijuana use has decreased among young people, domestic cultivation of the drug seems to be on the rise. Government estimates claim that approximately 50,000 metric tons of marijuana were grown in the United States in 1989, continuing the pattern of steady annual increases.

Some attribute the surge in domestic cultivation to the shortage of imported marijuana, the result of improved efforts to stop the drug from entering the United States. Others cite the "paraquat scares" of the late 1970s, in which imported marijuana was found to be contaminated with that herbicide, leading determined users either to grow their own or to purchase only from local growers. Few dispute that the sky-rocketing cost of marijuana—from less than $200 for the most potent varieties in the late 1970s to many hundreds of dollars for the highest grade in the early 1990s—has made the practice of growing cannabis far more lucrative.

Foreign Effects

The economies of many nations have been seriously affected by the cultivation of marijuana and other drugs. In countries such as Colombia and Mexico (the two leading sources of imported marijuana in the United States), farmers facing economic hardship must decide whether to grow legal crops (such as coffee) or cannabis, which can earn them much more money. At the same time, foreign governments, worried about their constituents as well as about the threat of direct retribution by well-armed drug cartels, are often reluctant to assist American efforts at stopping local production.

Marijuana-Related Businesses

As a result of the trend toward domestic marijuana cultivation, a subindustry that markets sophisticated growing equipment designed for producing marijuana indoors has developed. Mail-order houses and gardening stores sell elaborate hydroponic systems (which permit plants to be grown without soil), grow lamps, and climate control devices, marketed more or less discreetly for the purpose of growing cannabis. A number of books are available that offer agricultural tips to growers; *High Times* magazine, begun in 1974, continues to represent the underground marijuana culture in its various forms.

Paraphernalia

In addition, since its heyday in the late 1970s, the so-called paraphernalia industry has remained afloat despite various governmental efforts to curb its growth. *Paraphernalia* is the term used for the myriad devices marketed to marijuana users, such as certain brands of cigarette rolling paper, cigarette rolling machines, smoking pipes (including *hookahs* and *bongs*), devices for holding marijuana cigarettes (*roach clips* and *roach stones*), equipment for removing seeds and stems from marijuana, various types of storage containers, and scales for measuring the substance (usually in grams or fractions of an ounce).

Despite its continued existence, however, marijuana paraphernalia is no longer as widely available as it once was. Rolling paper can still be purchased at almost any store that sells cigarettes, but water pipes and other items more obviously intended for marijuana smoking are available only in select novelty shops. The *head shop* of the 1960s and 1970s, a store devoted specifically to selling drug paraphernalia, along with posters, logo T-shirts, and other items linked to the drug culture, is largely a thing of the past because of community opposition and local law enforcement efforts.

(continued from page 43)

tolerance policy adopted under the Reagan administration supports extreme punitive measures for all marijuana-related crime, from use to trafficking. In addition to fines and imprisonment, the policy permits the seizure of individual assets, including homes, cars, and bank accounts. The forfeiture of personal property for legal infractions dates back to the English common law of the Middle Ages. Although forfeiture of estate was forbidden under a statute passed by the first U.S. Congress, these procedures were changed during the Civil War, and drug offenders today are still subject to property seizure. Money seized in this manner generally goes to fund drug enforcement efforts; in some states, such as New York, the money is directed toward drug prevention and education.

Destroying Home-Grown Crops A subset of the DCE/SP, Operation Green Merchant, is an ongoing effort targeting

An American soldier buys illicit drugs from a Vietnamese woman along a highway in South Vietnam in 1971. The easy availability of such substances led to widespread use among U.S. military personnel during the Vietnam War, despite combined antidrug campaigns by the Vietnamese and American governments.

indoor home growers, as well as suppliers of home gardening equipment and seeds. Names of shippers and customers have been obtained from United Parcel Service records and other sources to locate domestic growers, and the DEA has been working to extradite persons involved with shipping active, high-grade marijuana seeds into the United States. (Most mail-order companies providing these seeds are located in Holland.) In 1989, 441 people were arrested, 48,744 sinsemilla plants and almost one ton of processed marijuana were destroyed in 356 indoor operations, and $9 million in property and assets were seized.

Another effort, the Campaign Against Marijuana Planting (CAMP), is a federal, state, and local program dealing specifically with crop eradication in California. Launched in the early 1980s, CAMP initiatives often make use of thermal video systems to locate the intense heat emitted by high-wattage grow lights within suspected buildings. Another strategy used to locate indoor growing operations is checking electric bills because multiple grow-light setups draw a very large amount of electric current.

Drug Testing

In addition to punitive action, such as fines and imprisonment, urine testing for evidence of marijuana use has become another way to deter individuals from using the drug. Such testing has become routine for prospective employees in many companies, for military recruits, and for professional and student athletes. In 1989, the U.S. Bureau of Labor Statistics reported that 20% of those employed in the United States work for companies that enforce some sort of drug testing.

Although no one would claim that going to school or work under the influence of drugs or alcohol is a good idea—especially if an individual uses machinery or operates a vehicle—drug testing remains a controversial practice. Test results indicating marijuana use can mean the loss of a job, establishment of a permanent record as a drug user, and forced entry into treatment programs. In most cases, job candidates who test positive for marijuana or other drugs are not considered for employment.

Those who support drug testing do so for several reasons. Some believe that people who use drugs are crying out for help and that this is one way to determine who they are. Others feel that marijuana use in the workplace and at school threatens everyone's safety, costs businesses money through increased absenteeism and reduced productivity, and—because of marijuana's effects on memory (see Chapter 5)— impedes the educational process.

In response, the American Civil Liberties Union and others who oppose urine testing say the practice violates individual civil rights guaranteed by the Fourth Amendment's protection from unreasonable search and seizure. As for costs to the educational system and business world, they believe that an individual's actual job or school performance should be assessed—not his or her leisure time activities. As of early 1991, eight states had drug-testing laws that included provisions to protect employees from the negative consequences of random testing by requiring reasonable suspicion of drug use, confidentiality of results, privacy during the test, and a subsequent test for accuracy in the event of a positive result (that is, one indicating drug use).

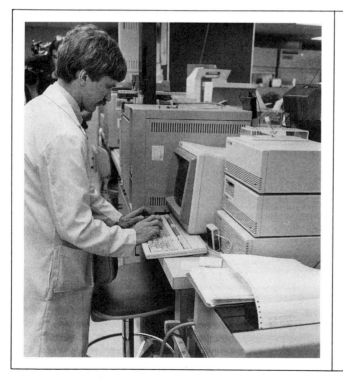

Dr. Barry Sample, assistant director of the Sports Medicine Drug Identification Laboratory at the Indiana University School of Medicine, inspects one of the devices used to test athletes competing in the 1987 Pan-American Games in Indianapolis. During the 1980s increasing numbers of participants in major sports events were tested for the use of both legal and illegal drugs.

In 1989, the U.S. Supreme Court ruled on the constitutionality of testing government employees not suspected of drug use. Even though the Court held that urine testing amounts to a search, it found that the government's desire for a drug-free work force outweighs the constitutional right to privacy.

A Question of Accuracy Not only is the use of urine tests controversial, but debate rages over whether the tests themselves are reliable. Because the tests are not 100% accurate, some individuals may test positive even if they do not use drugs and some may test negative even if they do. Depending on one's school of thought, false positives mean that "innocent" people are being punished unnecessarily, although to others the possibility of a false negative raises the specter of "guilty" people passing the test scot-free. Inaccurate results pose a particular risk if there is no second test performed to double-check the first result.

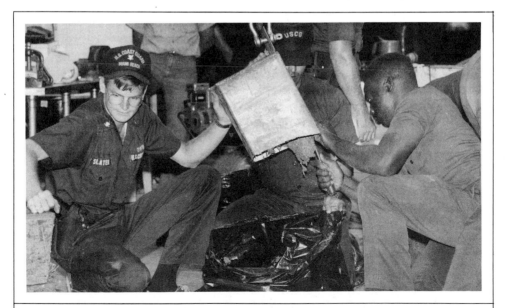

U.S. Coastguardsmen remove marijuana from one of four steel boxes found attached to the hull of a cruise ship in June 1990 at the Port of Miami. Officials arrested two divers and an accomplice as they swam under the ship in an effort to retrieve the smuggled drug.

Moreover, because vestiges of THC can linger in the body for 30 days or more, many argue that urine tests are biased against marijuana users. Only very recent cocaine or heroin use is detected because these substances are eliminated from the body much faster than marijuana. A number of people also believe that cocaine and heroin have a greater negative impact on society than does marijuana and that the drug-testing effort is therefore misplaced.

The Miami Case In what its opponents consider a related breach of employee civil rights, on January 23, 1991, the Miami Beach City Commission approved an ordinance that requires the police to report a drug arrest to the accused's employer. This measure is the first of its kind in the nation. Though a draft of the notification letter warns employers not to punish workers and recommends drug counseling and rehabilitation, those who oppose the measure fear that people are likely to lose their job and will face difficulty being hired in the future. The measure is supported by the DEA, the U.S. Customs Service, the Bureau of Alcohol, Tobacco and Firearms, and some local doctors and educators.

Decriminalization

Effects on Marijuana Use An essential aspect of the debate over penalties for marijuana use is concern over the effect decriminalization has on the drug's consumption. Two states, California and Ohio, collected data on the subject both before and after decriminalization. In California, where marijuana was decriminalized in January 1976, use in adults rose 7% between February 1975 and November 1976. In Ohio, where marijuana was decriminalized in November 1975, use in 18 to 24 year olds rose 6% between 1974 and 1978. During the same time period, use among 25 to 34 year olds went up 13%.

However, a Canadian study of marijuana use trends in the United States reanalyzed four national surveys performed between 1972 and 1977 and concluded that rates of marijuana use in the states that had decriminalized it were higher than those of other states even before the laws were changed. Although in the aftermath of reduced penalties there was increased use, the rise was actually less than the rate of increase during the same time period in states that had retained more severe penalties.

Another study compared marijuana use in four Michigan communities. In one of these, Ann Arbor, marijuana laws had changed four times: from prohibition to reduced penalties; to decriminalization; to recriminalization; and finally to decriminalization again. Meanwhile, the other three communities strictly prohibited marijuana. After comparing marijuana use in the four areas, researchers found that use rates in Ann Arbor appeared to be unaffected by changes in the local law.

Decriminalization in Holland Evidence from other countries also supports the idea that harsh drug penalties may not alleviate the problem. In 1976, the Dutch government decriminalized marijuana. Though the substance is illegal, users are not punished, and more than 100 cafés in

As an armed special agent of the U.S. Bureau of Land Management (BLM) watches (lower left), BLM director Cy Jamison and an officer in the California National Guard rip out a marijuana plant found growing deep in the public forestlands of California's Humboldt County in the summer of 1990. The raid destroyed 1,200 plants producing potent sinsemilla marijuana, and 5 tons of equipment used to maintain the "guerrilla garden" were seized, but no arrests were made. Since the 1970s, illicit cultivation of marijuana in remote areas of both private and public lands has become widespread.

Amsterdam are tacitly allowed to sell hashish and marijuana over the counter. This system has divided the drug market into two distinct segments: the freely operating "soft drug" marijuana market and the "hard drug" black market, consisting mostly of heroin. The so-called gateway effect of marijuana's leading to harder drugs can be viewed partly as a consequence of the black-market drug dealer's economic incentive to hook a marijuana user on a more expensive and addictive drug such as heroin. The Dutch system apparently helps to circumvent this problem by effectively taking marijuana off the black market.

Street dealers are reported to still sell marijuana, mainly to unsuspecting tourists and to others seeking the substance when the commercial outlets are closed. By and large, however, users can purchase marijuana of a known quality in the clubs and cafés and, therefore, stay away from street dealers. Moreover, between 1976 and 1986 there was actually a decrease in marijuana use, from 10% to 6%, among 17 to 18 year olds in Holland.

Legalization

Were it made fully legal, marijuana would most likely be subject to the same prohibitions and social taboos as alcohol: no sale to those under 18 years of age and no driving while intoxicated. The government might also license and tax its growth, importation, distribution, and sale. Legalization of marijuana would also reestablish the nation's use of the cannabis plant for ecologically sound paper, as well as for textiles, food, and fuel.

Those who support legalization cite many reasons for their viewpoint. They argue that outlawing the drug not only seems to have little or no effect but actually does more harm than good because it results in criminal activity and the creation of a black market. In addition, they say the lack of quality control makes marijuana use more dangerous because the user does not know how potent the product is or whether it has been mixed with other substances. Moreover, those who want marijuana to be legalized claim that the amount of time and money spent on law enforcement is excessive, given what they perceive to be the substance's relatively mild effect.

In an open letter to William Bennett (who at that time was the director of the Office of National Drug Control Policy), Nobel Prize–winning economist Milton Friedman supported marijuana legalization as an economic solution to an economic problem. According to an article in the *Wall Street Journal* in September 1989, Friedman stated that illegal marijuana means, among other things, that drug lords profit from its cultivation and sale and that law enforcement energies are diverted from other efforts. A December 1989 poll by the *Los Angeles Times* said that 30% of Americans surveyed favor decriminalization.

Although William Bennett told the Associated Press in December 1989 that marijuana was no more dangerous than alcohol, he was against legalization. Bennett stated, "The last thing I would want to do is recommend the wider use of a drug that makes young people stupid." In contrast, public figures supporting legalization include conservative journalist William F. Buckley, Jr., scientist Carl Sagan, and former New York City Police Commissioner Patrick V. Murphy.

An official in the law enforcement office of the U.S. Forest Service displays sample booby traps used by marijuana growers. The traps, equipped with trip wires attached to firearms, pipe bombs, and hand grenades, are used to protect crops grown illicitly in national forests.

A poster from the U.S. Department of Health and Human Services urges would-be users of marijuana and other drugs to Just Say No, a slogan that became the theme of the government's war against drugs in the 1980s.

CHAPTER 4

TRENDS AND ATTITUDES

Most studies show that marijuana use has not remained constant during the drug's recent history in the United States. Reports of its prevalence have fluctuated along with society's attitudes toward the substance. Roughly speaking, marijuana use increased in the 1960s and 1970s, when public opinion held that it was a largely harmless drug, and decreased in the 1980s and early 1990s in response to an increased concern over the use of all drugs.

How Many People Use Marijuana?

According to the *1988 National Household Survey* on drug abuse, conducted by NIDA, approximately 66 million Americans aged 12 and up have tried marijuana at least once in their life. The figure breaks down to about 4 million (or 17% of) young Americans aged 12 to 17; 17 million (or 56% of) young adults aged 18 to 25; and 45 million (or 31% of) adults aged 26 and up. Among all of these groups, it was estimated that 5.5 million people used the drug once a week or more.

Even so, marijuana use among young people actually seems to be on the decline. For example, the *Household Survey* indicates that between 1972 and 1979, the number of Americans between 12 and 25 years old who had used marijuana at least once in their life rose steadily to a peak in

1979. That means that by the end of the 1970s, 31% of Americans aged 12 to 17 years old and 68% of those aged 18 to 25 years old had tried pot. However, from that point through the 1988 survey, as the previous figures show, marijuana became steadily less popular among these age groups.

The same cannot be said, though, for adults aged 26 and up. Instead, marijuana use among these individuals increased over the years, from fewer than 20% in 1979 to 31% in 1988. The continued rise is attributed to the the large number of people in this group who began using marijuana when they were younger.

However, the number of people currently using marijuana (that is, those who had used the drug at least once in the month prior to being surveyed) declined in all age groups. The survey estimated that more than 6% of young people aged 12 to 17 were current users in 1988, compared to a peak of 17% in 1979. For young adults aged 18 to 25, the figure was almost 16% in 1988, compared to more than 35% in 1979. Finally, 4% of adults aged 26 and up were current users in 1988, compared to a peak of almost 7% in 1982.

Because this type of survey is difficult to perform, however, NIDA's studies may understate the number of people who actually use marijuana. NORML, for example, refutes NIDA's findings and instead estimates that in the late 1980s about 30 million Americans used marijuana at least once a week.

Nonetheless, the downward trend in use of the drug during the 1980s has been indicated in research other than the *Household Survey*. A series of reports issued by the Gordon S. Black Corporation, an independent market research and polling firm, also shows that marijuana use has become less prevalent. Surveys conducted by the company in the late 1980s noted a 28% decrease in the number of American teenagers who reported using marijuana at least once in the year prior to the survey. The number of adults reporting similar use decreased 26% during the same period.

In its 1989 findings, the University of Michigan, which conducts annual surveys of drug use among both high school and college students, offered further indications that national marijuana use was in decline. The number of high school seniors surveyed who had used marijuana in the month before the survey declined from 37% in 1979 to 17% in 1989.

Between 1980 and 1989, use among college students in a similar presurvey period declined from 34% to 16%. The proportional drop in daily use was even greater for both populations.

Other factors in the decreased prevalence of marijuana use may include cost and lack of availability. Although the 1989 University of Michigan survey showed that large proportions of high school and college students felt marijuana was "readily available," some sources in 1990 reported a scarcity of marijuana on the black market, perhaps a result of increased efforts to seize and eradicate the drug. The price of an ounce of marijuana (enough for about 40 cigarettes) ran between about $25 and $175 (depending on the potency) in the late 1970s, but by the early 1990s, users commonly paid a few hundred dollars, according to *High Times*.

Attitudes Toward Use

Concurrent with the drop in marijuana use during the 1980s have been a reversal of tolerance toward the drug's use and an increased perception that it can pose real dangers. According to NIDA's *1988 National High School Senior Survey*, 77% of graduating high school seniors saw a "great risk" in smoking marijuana regularly, up from about 70% in the 1985 survey. According to the University of Michigan studies, the percentage of high school seniors who perceived "great risk" in using marijuana only once or twice had increased from 9.4% in 1979 to 23.6% in 1989.

Another report, the *Partnership Attitude Tracking Study* (PATS), is a large attitudinal study of drug abuse conducted by the Gordon S. Black Corporation in cooperation with the Partnership for a Drug-Free America and funded by NIDA. It documented a notable shift in attitudes toward marijuana use between 1987 and 1990.

Seventy percent of adults surveyed by PATS in 1990 felt there was "moderate" or "great" risk in occasional marijuana use, as opposed to 66% in 1987. Between 1989 and 1990, the percentage of teenagers surveyed who held similar beliefs rose from 64% to 72%. The perceived use of marijuana by peer group members appears to have declined as well. In addition, 39% of adults surveyed in 1990 said they had friends who were occasional marijuana users, down from 45% in 1987. A similar shift was noted among preteens (9% in 1990,

A poster in the late 1970s advertises a special showing of the 1936 film Reefer Madness, a sensationalistic "exposé" of the alleged dangers of marijuana use. Today the film's simpleminded scare tactics seem more comical than instructive.

compared to 14% in 1987) as well as among teenagers (47% in 1990, compared to 56% in 1989).

These responses appeared consistent along racial lines. Fifty-six percent of black adults surveyed in 1987 said they had friends who used marijuana occasionally; in 1990, that percentage dropped to 50%. In addition, 43% of white adults reporting in 1987 made similar claims, compared with 37% in 1990.

Shaping Opinions The power of the media to influence public attitudes has long been recognized, and its use in shaping opinions on drug use is not new. The film *Reefer Madness* was part of a widespread antimarijuana campaign during the 1930s, one that included an increased number of articles in U.S. newspapers that supposedly documented the dangers of the drug.

During the 1960s and 1970s, increased public tolerance of marijuana use was reflected—and possibly encouraged— by news footage of hippies and others smoking marijuana without major consequence. Use of the drug was extolled directly and indirectly in popular music (Brewer and Shipley's 1971 Top 10 hit "One Toke over the Line" and the New Riders of the Purple Sage's "Panama Red" are two of the more blatant examples) and by musicians and other celebrities. A school of comedy often referred to as drug humor, epitomized by performers such as Cheech and Chong, poked fun at drug (particularly marijuana) use and drug users. By the late 1970s and early 1980s, it was not uncommon to see a character in a major motion picture smoke a joint in the same way one might sip a glass of wine in a casual social setting. Marijuana use had, by some standards, become "normalized" in American society.

During the 1980s, however, efforts began to "denormalize" the use of marijuana and other drugs in the United States. The media began featuring more news stories, features, editorials, and specials that focused on the country's drug problem. At the same time, TV and movie producers began making a conscious effort to deglamorize drug use, either by not portraying it or by showing drug use to have pronounced negative effects. Many popular musicians, in both a renewed commitment to social activism and a rejection of 1960s stereotypes, came out against drug use in the 1980s.

Along with these media trends, there was a stepped-up and increasingly sophisticated use of advertising aimed at shifting attitudes toward marijuana and other drugs. The most notable effort has been that of the Partnership for a Drug-Free America, a nonprofit coalition of volunteers from the advertising, public relations, research, and media industries that was formed in 1986.

The Partnership's goal has been to reduce demand for illegal drugs by using media communication—specifically advertising—to encourage intolerance of drug use and drug users by the American public. Between 1987 and 1990, the group produced more than 250 antidrug messages for print, radio, and television. These were aimed specifically at groups such as children, teenagers, parents of teenagers, and expectant mothers. Minority groups, including blacks and Hispanics, have also been targeted. These ads are designed to

Poet Allen Ginsberg leads a group of demonstrators in New York City in 1965 calling for the legalization of marijuana.

discourage drug experimentation among nonusers, to increase perceived risk of use among occasional users, and to encourage parents, employers, and health care professionals to actively discourage drug use among those they can influence.

The organization's efforts appear to have been effective in changing attitudes and behavior with regard to marijuana and other drugs. The PATS research carried out between 1987 and 1990, the first three years of the Partnership's campaign, noted a marked reduction in drug use and a parallel increase in antidrug attitudes in areas of the nation where Partnership ads were prominent.

Factors Leading to Antidrug Sentiments A number of events have contributed to the current backlash against drug use in the United States. Perhaps foremost has been the

Antidrug activists march in New York City in the 1970s.

role played by crack. A rise in crime rates in major cities has been attributed directly to crack use because people hooked on this highly addictive drug apparently seek to support their habit through theft and robbery. At the same time, a new class of drug dealers has evolved, lured into the business of selling crack by the ease with which the drug can be produced and by a vast potential for profit. Battles for control of lucrative sales districts between heavily armed gangs have resulted in numerous deaths.

Another factor fueling public opinion against drugs has been the issue of drug use in the workplace. Intoxication, as a result of using either drugs or alcohol, is thought to have played a part in a spate of widely publicized industrial and public transportation accidents.

William Bennett, then head of the U.S. government's war on drugs, speaks to students at a middle school in Miami in 1989. During his term as the nation's "drug czar," Bennett called for the elimination of drugs in all schools, as well as the imposition of more severe penalties against drug dealers.

The prevalence of AIDS among intravenous drug users has also had an impact on people's perception of drug use in general. In addition, the trend toward political and religious conservatism in the United States has recast the national drug question in terms of morality.

All of these factors have affected the country's views on marijuana use. For better or for worse, marijuana is no longer seen as the harmless plant many considered it to be in the 1960s and 1970s. Instead, it has once again become a symbol of a wider national drug problem.

Attitudes Toward Drug Laws

In 1977, a Gallup poll of the general population showed that 28% of those surveyed supported legalization of marijuana and that 66% opposed it. In 1985, a similar Gallup poll found that only 23% of respondents still supported legalization and that 73% were opposed to it.

Opinion on decriminalization was more equally divided, according to the 1985 study. Although 46% of those surveyed believed that possession of small amounts of marijuana should not be treated as a criminal offense, 50% felt that it should. Previous polls in 1977 and 1980 had shown a small majority of respondents supporting decriminalization.

Although support for decriminalization seemed to be waning in the late 1980s in light of general antidrug sentiment, the issue was revived by some members of the legal and law enforcement professions because of crowded prisons and overflowing court dockets.

In a survey of 181 chief drug prosecutors or their deputies throughout the United States carried out by the *National Law Journal* and published in August 1988, a majority placed marijuana in a category different from that for heroin, cocaine, crack, and phencyclidine (PCP); almost 75% rejected the zero-tolerance policy; and 25% said they believed marijuana should be decriminalized.

A young boy smokes marijuana at an annual "hash bash" attended by his parents in Ann Arbor, Michigan, in the early 1970s. Smoking marijuana has many of the same health risks as cigarette smoking.

CHAPTER 5

MARIJUANA AND HEALTH

Since the 1920s, researchers in the United States and other countries have sought to determine the full extent of health risks posed by marijuana use. In 1925, the U.S. Army released a study on soldiers stationed in the Panama Canal Zone, among whom marijuana use was prevalent. The report concluded that the drug was neither habit forming nor dangerous; the army reiterated this position in 1933. In 1938, Mayor Fiorello LaGuardia of New York commissioned a study that was performed by the New York Academy of Medicine and the New York City Police Department. Released in 1944, the LaGuardia report concluded that marijuana was not a gateway drug and that its potential social, medical, and psychological dangers had been vastly overestimated.

The National Institute of Mental Health began research on the effects of marijuana during the late 1960s. In 1972, Congress authorized the creation of the National Institute on Drug Abuse (NIDA), and NIDA research began in 1974. Because marijuana is illegal, there is public acceptance of the idea that it must significantly compromise physical health. Yet in many cases marijuana's effects on the body are still unknown.

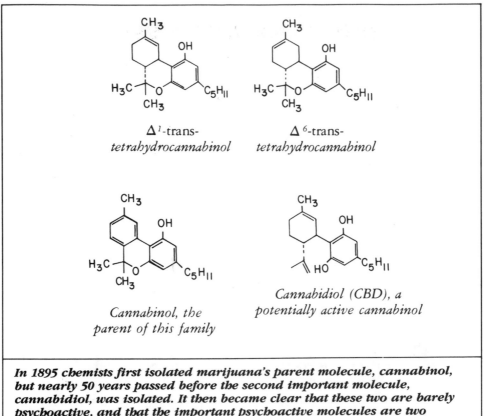

Δ¹-trans-
tetrahydrocannabinol

Δ⁶-trans-
tetrahydrocannabinol

*Cannabinol, the
parent of this family*

*Cannabidiol (CBD), a
potentially active cannabinol*

*In 1895 chemists first isolated marijuana's parent molecule, cannabinol,
but nearly 50 years passed before the second important molecule,
cannabidiol, was isolated. It then became clear that these two are barely
psychoactive, and that the important psychoactive molecules are two
variations of THC. As illustrated above, the subtle differences between the
molecules are due to the number and position of the double bonds, shown
here as two parallel lines.*

Marijuana's Path Through the Body

The effects of marijuana on the body and mind are believed
to be related to the dose of THC received, and that in turn
has to do with the quantity of marijuana used and its potency.
Although THC is only one of more than 400 chemicals in
marijuana, its potent mood-altering qualities make it the only
component to be widely studied.

When marijuana is smoked, THC enters the body
through the lungs; when marijuana is eaten, the chemical
enters via the stomach. Either way, it moves rapidly through
the bloodstream and into the brain, as well as into most of
the body's tissues and organs. Excess THC is stored in body

fat, metabolized by the liver, and slowly excreted through feces and urine. However, THC leaves the body so slowly that, as discussed earlier, a regular marijuana smoker's urine may test positive for more than four weeks after the last time the individual used the drug.

Health Risks

For all that is still uncertain about marijuana's effects, one thing is clear: At least part of the health risk associated with the drug's use stems from the fact that it is illegal and must be obtained on the black market, where there is no quality control or dosage standard. The strength of varying strains

Ask your doctor which of these is least harmful to your health.

Now ask your Congressman why it's illegal.

Nearly 490,000 Americans will die this year from accidents or illnesses related to alcohol or tobacco. But marijuana is no killer. In fact, medical evidence indicates many foods we commonly consume pose a greater danger to human health than marijuana. Still it remains illegal — consuming over $5 billion of our tax dollars for law enforcement each year. But if regulated, marijuana sales would generate $10 to $15 billion dollars in annual tax revenue.

It could be you.
400,000 people are arrested each year on marijuana charges — 85% of

them for simple possession. If you enjoy occasional recreational use, this fact should trouble you. Because while these laws remain on the books you're in jeopardy. You risk social and financial disaster. In many states you can still be sent to prison for possessing even a small quantity of pot. Now consider that because of the escalating "War on Drugs," penalties for marijuana possession are being severely increased — putting you at greater risk than ever before.

Send a buck.
Whether you smoke marijuana often, occasionally, *or not at all*, you

should be angry about its prohibition. Why not join N.O.R.M.L. — the National Organization for the Reform of Marijuana Laws? Membership is only $25.00. If you're skittish about sending us your name, just drop a buck in the mail to:

N.O.R.M.L.
*2001 "S" Street, NW, Suite 640
Washington, DC 20009
(202) 483 5500*

...or maybe 5 bucks, 10 bucks, or even 100 bucks. Your contribution will make a difference.

A poster from NORML, the National Organization for the Reform of Marijuana Laws, suggests that cigarettes and alcohol may be far worse for one's health than marijuana. In fact, serious health risks have been associated with all three drugs.

can differ widely and even experienced users have trouble knowing before they smoke the drug whether it contains other substances, such as PCP, crack, herbicides, or pesticides. Combining marijuana with other drugs can alter its effects and put the user at increased risk.

Effects on the Respiratory and Cardiovascular Systems

In an effort to determine its effects on the respiratory system, researchers often compare marijuana to tobacco, a substance posing fairly well known health risks. Because marijuana is not regulated by the government, however, the concentration of chemicals can vary greatly from one batch to another. Moreover, marijuana users tend to differ from cigarette smokers in terms of how much they smoke and how often. Both of these factors make comparisons between marijuana and tobacco difficult. Asthma, bronchitis, emphysema, heart disease, and lung cancer can all result from cigarette smoking but it is unclear whether equivalent exposure to marijuana will have similar results.

Nonetheless, although marijuana has not been proven to cause lung cancer, some researchers have linked pot smoking to precancerous lesions in the lungs. Moreover, irritation and obstruction of the upper airways (the sinuses and larynx) are frequent among users, and the lower airways (the trachea and bronchi) may also become irritated, resulting in a sore throat and cough. Heavy marijuana use may compromise the lungs' ability to clean and repair themselves.

Marijuana also speeds up the heart rate, increasing the need for oxygen. At the same time, smoking reduces the amount of oxygen available to the heart and stresses the cardiovascular system. Therefore, despite remaining questions concerning marijuana's health risks, individuals who suffer from heart disease and high blood pressure definitely should not use the drug.

Marijuana Smoke and Toxins Both marijuana smoke and tobacco smoke contain toxic chemicals, and research performed at the University of California, Los Angeles, sought to compare the effects of these types of smoke on the lungs. Although the chemical content can vary from one batch of marijuana to the next, based on the samples used the scientists found that smoking marijuana causes five times more carbon monoxide to accumulate in the blood than smoking cigarettes does. The researchers also concluded that three times more tar is inhaled from marijuana smoke than from cigarette smoke and that one-third more tar settles into the respiratory tract. The potential respiratory damage from one joint was judged similar to that of five cigarettes. The nature of marijuana use—which includes inhaling deeply and holding the smoke in the lungs for a maximum high—contribute to the effects on the lungs.

In fact, research performed at the Johns Hopkins University School of Medicine found evidence that users adjust their smoking behavior depending on the marijuana's THC content and smoke less as the potency increases. On this basis, some scientists believe that more potent marijuana may actually present less of a risk to the lungs of pot smokers than does lower-grade marijuana. If people smoke less and, therefore, inhale less, they are likely to do less damage to their lungs.

Aside from toxins present in the plant material itself, marijuana can also contain harmful contaminants. *Salmonella* bacteria or *aspergillus* fungi may infest marijuana and cause lung infections in smokers. In one case, the University of California San Francisco Medical Center reported that despite the administration of antifungal medication, aspergillus infection proved fatal to a heavy marijuana user whose immune system was temporarily impaired following a bone marrow transplant for leukemia.

Marijuana's Effects on the Immune System
Marijuana may temporarily depress the immune system, especially the production of T lymphocytes, those white blood cells that help the body resist viruses and fight cancer. In a recent study at the University of South Florida, marijuana was shown to weaken the ability of white blood cells to fight tumor cells under certain conditions. Whether this phenomenon significantly increases the risk of cancer and other diseases in users has not been determined.

Marijuana's Effects on Fertility
Heavy use of marijuana may affect the endocrine, or hormonal, systems of both men and women. In males, early studies indicated reduced

levels of testosterone (a male hormone), lowered sperm count, impotence, and gynecomastia (development of the mammary glands in men). Research also found disrupted menstrual cycles in women.

Much about marijuana's effects on fertility is still unknown. However, a Costa Rican study of long-term marijuana smokers who had begun using the substance in their teens found that though sperm count and testosterone levels did drop, there was no measurable effect on libido or fertility among the subjects.

Marijuana's Effects on Pregnancy Because alcohol and tobacco have been shown to cause complications during pregnancy and labor and to contribute to below-average birth weight in babies, much research has focused on the effects of marijuana on pregnancy.

Even so, attempting to determine whether or not marijuana use during pregnancy leads to birth defects is difficult

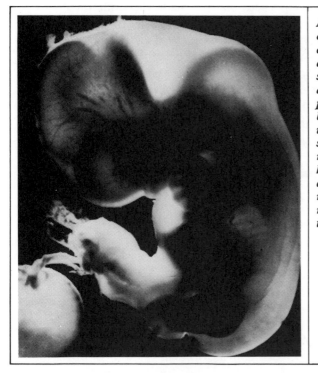

A 45-day-old human embryo, which is at a critical point in its development, is extremely sensitive to any external agents that cross the placenta; some can cause birth defects. A pregnant woman who smokes any substance, including marijuana, faces serious health hazards. The drug's effects include the reduction of oxygen in the mother's blood that leads to retarded fetal growth.

because it is unethical to provide drugs to pregnant women on an experimental basis. Instead, subjects provide researchers with information on their own drug use throughout the course of their pregnancy. There are several drawbacks to this method, however, including the questionable accuracy of information provided by the women surveyed and the wide variation in the potency of the marijuana used.

When evaluating marijuana's effects on an unborn child, researchers assess many different aspects of the pregnancy and compare them to those of mothers who do not use the drug. These aspects include the length of the gestation period (that is, how long the fetus remains in the womb before a woman gives birth), the duration of labor, the newborn's weight and length, the presence of birth defects, and in some cases follow-up assessment as the child matures.

The Ottawa Prenatal Prospective Study, headed by psychologist P. A. Fried, suggests that heavy marijuana use during pregnancy (five or more marijuana cigarettes per week) results in shorter gestation and an increased risk of two types of birth defects. One is *ocular hypertelorism*, an abnormally wide spacing of the eyes. This syndrome is accompanied by mental retardation in some infants. The other is *epicanthus*, a defect of the eyelid characterized by an extra, misplaced fold of skin.

Other studies, however, including one recently performed at the Johns Hopkins School of Medicine, have found that there is no substantial evidence linking marijuana alone to birth defects or premature birth (giving birth before the end of the full nine-month gestation period). These researchers believe that previous studies linking marijuana use to defects did not differentiate between women who used only marijuana and those who used marijuana in addition to smoking cigarettes and using other drugs, including alcohol, cocaine, heroin, or PCP.

Research by psychologist Ernest L. Abel further suggests that other reports have not properly accounted for the effects of malnutrition and poor general health status both before and during pregnancy among the women studied. Abel's work with pregnant rats has shown that a healthy diet can negate some of the effects that marijuana exposure might otherwise have on offspring.

However, some researchers have come across significant, though temporary, differences in the behavior patterns and nervous systems of infants born to women who frequently used marijuana during their pregnancy and in those of infants born to women who did not use the drug. Studies by Fried found that infants born to women who smoked more than two marijuana cigarettes per week during their pregnancy were less responsive to stimuli, less able to eventually quiet themselves down when crying, more likely to suffer tremors, easier to startle, and typified by a high-pitched cry—all signs of an immature nervous system. Yet one month after birth these characteristics were no longer apparent—raising the possibility that the infants' neurological development had caught up.

On the other hand, a study using subjects from the prenatal clinics (centers that oversee the health of pregnant

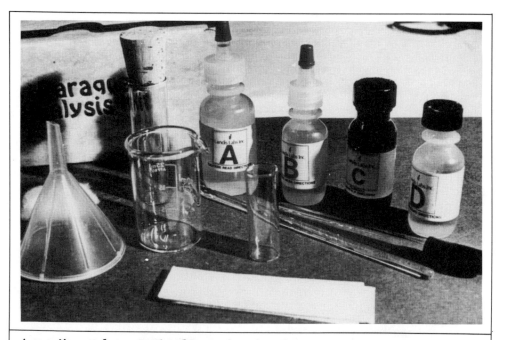

A marijuana home-testing kit marketed in the late 1970s to detect the presence of the herbicide paraquat. Paraquat damages many body organs, including the lungs, heart, kidneys, adrenal glands, and brain; people who smoke marijuana contaminated with paraquat risk injury to these organs.

women) at Denver General and University Hospitals found that women who used marijuana during their pregnancy gained more weight than those who did not, a condition that can arguably mean a more successful pregnancy. Interestingly, there was an overall ratio of two male babies to every female baby born to subjects who used marijuana three or more times weekly. Significantly smaller babies were born to women who smoked three or more joints a day during the first trimester, yet one year later there were no developmental differences between toddlers born to marijuana users and those born to nonusers. The impact of marijuana use by breast-feeding mothers on their children is still unclear. Though THC can be transmitted in breast milk, the small number of toddlers in this category of the study showed no developmental problems.

Marijuana's Effects on the Brain Though some researchers in the early 1970s reported that marijuana use might kill brain cells, other scientists challenged these findings. It is a fact, however, that concentration and reaction are impaired when an individual is intoxicated. Physical coordination is also temporarily affected.

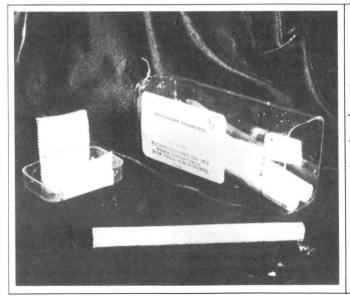

The U.S. government cultivates its own marijuana crops for research and medical purposes. Shown here is a sample of legal joints made from cannabis plants grown at the University of Mississippi.

In addition, many studies have shown that frequent marijuana use can impair short-term memory. This impairment occurs because the drug inhibits the release in the brain of a chemical known as *acetylcholine*, which transmits signals from one brain cell to another. One study of adolescent marijuana users in an outpatient drug abuse treatment program in Washington, D.C., showed that short-term memory deficits lasted at least six weeks after the last episode of marijuana use.

Another negative effect attributed to marijuana use is *amotivational syndrome*, or loss of motivation, a set of behavior problems that includes lack of concern about the future; lessening of ambition, drive, and will; diminished physical activity; apathy; and self-neglect.

Roger Roffman, author of Marijuana as Medicine *and* Using Marijuana in the Reduction of Nausea Associated with Chemotherapy, *was also the first person to study the widespread use of marijuana by servicemen in Vietnam. It is estimated that 10% to 20% used marijuana regularly.*

Research findings regarding this effect are contradictory. Although there were studies performed through the late 1960s that attributed amotivational syndrome to marijuana use, these are considered flawed because they did not take into account each subject's personality characteristics before he or she initially used the drug. That flaw makes it unclear which came first, amotivational tendencies or marijuana use. Current research suggests that, indeed, amotivational syndrome probably has more to do with an individual's personality than with pot. Moreover, Jamaican and Colombian studies show that in some cases marijuana use may actually increase work output and motivation when an individual performs certain boring or monotonous jobs.

In other cases, marijuana has been correlated with low levels of social achievement, criminal activity, higher college drop-out rates, and use of other drugs and alcohol. Again, however, even though abuse of the substance may make existing emotional problems worse, whether marijuana can actually cause antisocial behavior or psychological problems has not been proven.

Nonetheless, studies during the 1970s of test subjects engaged in both simulated and actual driving, as well as in simulated flying, have shown that marijuana impairs perception of time, distance, and coordination.

Phoenix House, a drug rehabilitation center, considers education an integral element of its treatment program. Here, in a public high school, a Phoenix House staff member conducts a class on drug use.

CHAPTER 6

PREVENTION AND TREATMENT OF MARIJUANA ABUSE

Although criminal punishment has served as a longtime strategy against drug abuse, another approach relies on education and training programs, as well as on medically and psychologically based treatment.

Defining Dependence and Abuse

The thrust of prevention and treatment of marijuana abuse depends on how society perceives dependence and abuse, a perception that is subject to change with the social climate. In the 1970s, marijuana was considered relatively benign, the younger generation's equivalent to the alcohol freely imbibed by their parents. This was reflected by the number of state laws enacted to decriminalize the possession of small amounts of marijuana.

The current climate is less tolerant of social drugs, and even use of legal substances such as alcohol, cigarettes, and caffeine is often frowned upon. This climate, plus marijuana's illegal status, has led many people to consider any use of the drug as abuse—be it for recreation, for inclusion as part of a religious ceremony, or for help in easing the discomfort associated with many diseases. Another definition of abuse looks at how well an individual functions in daily life, meeting responsibilities at home, on the job, or at school and in relationships with others.

Table 1

Reported Use of Marijuana Among High School Seniors, 1975-1989

	Class Year					
	1975	1976	1977	1978	1979	1980
Percent reporting use at least once during lifetime	47.3	52.8	56.4	59.2	60.4	60.3
Percent reporting use in previous year	40.0	44.5	47.6	50.2	50.8	48.8
Percent reporting use in previous month	27.1	32.2	35.4	37.1	36.5	33.7
Percent reporting daily use in previous month	6.0	8.2	9.1	10.7	10.3	9.1

Source: National Institute on Drug Abuse

The American Psychiatric Association's *Diagnostic and Statistical Manual* defines cannabis dependence as daily or almost daily use of marijuana, accompanied by lethargy, an inability to feel pleasure, and problems with concentration and memory. Actual cannabis abuse is defined as episodic use that involves problem behavior, such as driving while high. Both disorders, according to the manual, include problems carrying out functions socially and on the job that cannot be attributed to other psychological or physical disorders. But such problems are considered to be less severe than the impairment seen with other drugs.

Marijuana dependence does not happen immediately but can develop through repeated use, as the amount of time an individual spends buying and using marijuana increases. Characteristics exhibited by heavy users include introversion, lack of drive, poor judgment, disorientation, and agitation. Marijuana may worsen preexisting psychiatric problems, partic-

Reported Use of Marijuana Among High School Seniors, 1975-1989								
Class Year								
1981	1982	1983	1984	1985	1986	1987	1988	1989
59.5	58.7	57.0	54.9	54.2	50.9	50.2	47.2	43.7
46.1	44.3	42.3	40.0	40.6	38.8	36.3	33.1	29.6
31.6	28.5	27.0	25.2	25.7	23.4	21.0	18.0	16.7
7.0	6.3	5.5	5.0	4.9	4.0	3.3	2.7	2.9

ularly those requiring treatment with prescribed mind-altering drugs.

Causes of Marijuana Use and Dependence

Adolescence is a tumultuous time during which young people leave childhood behind and learn to be adults. Increased freedom from parents is combined with other challenges, including dealing with hormonal changes and sexual development, coping with the pressures of dating, forming bonds with peers, doing well in school, and making plans for career and college. During these formative years, experimentation—with clothes, sex, and ideas—is a way of learning about the world. Experimentation with cigarettes, alcohol, and drugs is also common in adolescence; and many young people who try them do not develop dependence. Yet certain individuals appear to be more inclined than others to become drug dependent. Some experts believe that substance abuse results from a combination of social and psychological problems and is also partially influenced by society's reliance on caffeine, alcohol, and cigarettes, as well as on prescription and non-prescription drugs, in an attempt to make life more tolerable.

In addition, attitudes about drug use among preteens and teenagers are initially shaped by their family. When parents openly use cigarettes, prescription and over-the-counter drugs, illegal drugs, or alcohol, they may send a message to their children that these activities are acceptable. As youngsters become more independent, peers replace parents as role models, and friends' attitudes toward drug and alcohol use can play a major role in influencing individual standards and behavior.

Moreover, feelings of depression, anxiety, and low self-esteem, along with poor family relationships and trouble in school, may place an individual at higher risk for marijuana

This 1987 derailment of an Amtrak passenger train in Maryland killed 16 people and injured more than 100. Federal investigators concluded that the engineer, under the influence of marijuana, ignored signals that might have averted the disaster. In recent years numerous railway accidents have been attributed to marijuana use by engineers and other train personnel.

SLANG NAMES FOR MARIJUANA	
pot	hooch
reefer	doobie
spliff	grass
weed	gange (ganja)
nickel	sinse (sinsemilla)
joint	shake
roach	smoke
dime	maryjane
bone	Acapulco gold
buzz	Thai sticks
bong	hash
hit	

dependency. Unfortunately, continual marijuana use during the teen years is an escape from reality that can damage a young person's ability to face the problems of growing up and to forge an independent and meaningful life. Similar drug-related problems can occur after adolescence. Adults who chronically use marijuana often believe it improves their relationships, self-awareness, and daily functioning. However, researchers at the Center for Psychosocial Studies in New York City found that marijuana only insulated heavy users from the problems in their lives, robbing them of the ability to see reality clearly.

Impact in the Workplace and in School

Marijuana can impair motor coordination, perception of time and distance, concentration, and the ability to form coherent speech. For these reasons, those who use marijuana in a school or work setting are at a disadvantage in terms of performance and, in certain situations, may endanger themselves or others.

Effects of marijuana use at school and at work can range from an inability to follow a classroom demonstration to serious accidents such as the 1987 train collision in which 16 people were killed—an accident caused by an engineer who was under the influence of marijuana.

According to data from NIDA's 1988 *Household Survey*, of those Americans between 20 and 40 years of age holding full-time jobs, 22% had used an illegal drug within the year before being surveyed, and 12% had done so within the

Table 2

	Class of 1975	Class of 1976	Class of 1977	Class of 1978	Class of 1979
High School Seniors' Attitudes Toward Marijuana					
How much do you think people risk harming themselves (physically or in other ways) if they					
Try marijuana once or twice	15.1	11.4	9.5	8.1	9.4
Smoke marijuana occasionally	18.1	15.0	13.4	12.4	13.5
Smoke marijuana regularly	43.3	38.6	36.4	34.9	42.0
(Percentage saying "great risk")					
Do you disapprove of people (who are 18 or older)					
Trying marijuana once or twice	47.0	38.4	33.4	33.4	34.2
Smoking marijuana occasionally	54.8	47.8	44.3	43.5	45.3
Smoking marijuana regularly	71.9	69.5	65.5	67.5	69.2
(Percentage disapproving)					
Do you think that people (who are 18 or older) should be prohibited by law from					
Smoking marijuana in private	32.8	27.5	26.8	25.4	28.0
Smoking marijuana in public	63.1	59.1	58.7	59.5	61.8
(Percentage saying "yes")					
How do you think your close friends feel (or would feel) about your					
Trying marijuana once or twice	44.3	N.A.	41.8	N.A.	40.9
Smoking marijuana occasionally	54.8	N.A.	49.0	N.A.	48.2
Smoking marijuana regularly	75.0	N.A.	69.1	N.A.	70.2
(Percentage saying friends disapprove)					
How many of your friends would you estimate					
Smoke marijuana					
Percentage saying none:	17.0	17.1	14.1	13.9	12.4
Percentage saying most or all:	30.3	30.6	32.3	35.3	35.5
During the last 12 months how often have you been around people who use marijuana to get high or for "kicks"?					
Percentage saying not at all:	N.A.	20.5	19.0	17.3	17.0
Percentage saying often:	N.A.	32.5	37.0	39.0	38.9
How difficult do you think it would be to get marijuana if you wanted some?					
Percentage saying "fairly easy" or "very easy")	87.8	87.4	87.9	87.8	90.1

N.A. = Not available

Source: National Institute on Drug Abuse, National High School Senior Survey, "Monitoring the Future"

High School Seniors' Attitudes Toward Marijuana

Class of 1980	Class of 1981	Class of 1982	Class of 1983	Class of 1984	Class of 1985	Class of 1986	Class of 1987	Class of 1988	Class of 1989
10.0	13.0	11.5	12.7	14.7	14.8	15.1	18.4	19.0	23.6
14.7	19.1	18.3	20.6	22.6	24.5	25.0	30.4	31.7	36.5
50.4	57.6	60.4	62.8	66.9	70.4	71.3	73.5	77.0	77.5
39.0	40.0	45.5	46.3	49.3	51.4	54.6	56.6	60.8	64.6
49.7	52.6	59.1	60.7	63.5	65.8	69.0	71.6	74.0	77.2
74.6	77.4	80.6	82.5	84.7	85.5	86.6	89.2	89.3	89.8
28.9	35.4	36.6	37.8	41.6	44.7	43.8	47.6	51.8	51.5
66.1	67.4	72.8	73.6	75.2	78.2	78.9	79.7	81.3	80.0
42.6	46.4	50.3	52.0	54.1	54.7	56.7	58.0	62.9	63.7
50.6	55.9	57.4	59.9	62.9	64.2	64.4	67.0	72.1	71.1
72.0	75.0	74.7	77.6	79.2	81.0	82.3	82.9	85.5	84.9
13.6	17.0	15.6	19.7	22.3	20.5	20.8	21.6	24.7	27.5
31.3	27.7	23.8	21.7	18.3	19.8	18.2	15.8	13.6	13.4
18.0	19.8	22.1	23.8	25.6	26.5	28.0	29.6	33.0	35.2
33.8	33.1	28.0	26.1	24.8	24.2	24.0	20.6	17.9	19.5
89.0	89.2	88.5	86.2	84.6	85.5	85.2	84.8	85.0	84.3

previous month. This finding raises two issues: (1) what effect drug use has in the workplace, and (2) what role the workplace plays in treating drug abuse. There have been limited studies of drug abuse at the work site, and it is difficult to design and implement a controlled study in a work environment. This difficulty has resulted in a lack of information on the effects of marijuana use on health care costs as well as on factors affecting worker productivity, such as absenteeism, accidents, and injuries. (However, government estimates suggest that productivity losses may run into the billions of dollars annually.)

Nonetheless, a military report has indicated that the longer and more frequently an individual has used marijuana, the more likely it is that the person will be dismissed from military service on the basis of unsuitability. In addition, a study carried out by the U.S. Postal Service indicated that postal workers who tested positive for marijuana use at the

A poster encourages parents to help their children form a healthy "addiction"—to good books—rather than depending on drugs for stimulation.

time of their hiring had a "moderate" absentee rate 32% higher than that of individuals who tested negative for drug use. However, even when problems do arise among marijuana users, it can be unclear whether the drug is actually the source of the trouble.

Prevention of Marijuana Abuse

Increasing numbers of elementary, junior high, and senior high schools have incorporated drug education and prevention programs into their curriculum. These programs generally take one of two forms: *primary prevention* or *secondary prevention.*

Primary Prevention The goal of primary prevention is to prevent or delay the onset of experimental drug use—including the use of cigarettes, alcohol, and marijuana—among young people. A primary prevention program usually provides drug information and tries to help students acquire important skills in areas such as decision making and communication. The program also helps teach students how to refuse drugs, develop self-esteem, engage in self-improvement activities, and find drug-free ways to reduce stress.

Secondary Prevention Secondary prevention targets both experimental drug users (those who have used drugs infrequently in the past) and regular users. Secondary prevention has three main goals: (1) to prevent the transition from experimental use to regular use, (2) to prevent regular users from becoming problem or heavy users, and (3) to delay or prevent individuals who are taking one drug from starting to use a variety of other drugs as well. Programs aimed at secondary prevention usually combine the elements of primary prevention with group, peer, or individual counseling.

Prevention Strategies Of course, there is no magic formula for preventing drug abuse, but some strategies appear to be more successful than others. A technique used in both primary and secondary prevention programs is the *alternative activity* approach, which is based on the concept that persons provided with healthy, nonchemical ways of gaining pleasure and rewards—including art, music, sports, and other group- and community-oriented activities—are less likely to get involved in excessive use of drugs or alcohol. This method

Table 3

	Class of 1975	Class of 1976	Class of 1977	Class of 1978	Class of 1979
Trends in Seniors' Attitudes Toward Marijuana Laws					
(Entries are percentages)					
Q: There has been a great deal of public debate about whether marijuana use should be legal. Which of the following policies would you favor?					
Using marijuana should be entirely legal	27.3	32.6	33.6	32.9	32.1
It should be a minor violation like a parking ticket but not a crime	25.3	29.0	31.4	30.2	30.1
It should be a crime	30.5	25.4	21.7	22.2	24.0
Don't know	16.8	13.0	13.4	14.6	13.8
Q: If it were legal for people to USE marijuana should it also be legal to SELL marijuana?					
No	27.8	24.0	22.5	21.8	22.9
Yes, but only to adults	37.1	49.8	52.1	53.6	53.2
Yes, to anyone	16.2	13.3	12.7	12.0	11.3
Don't know	18.9	13.9	12.7	12.6	12.6
Q: If marijuana were legal to use and legally available, which of the following would you be most likely to do?					
Not use it, even if it were legal and available	53.2	50.4	50.6	46.4	50.2
Try it	8.2	8.1	7.0	7.1	6.1
Use it about as often as I do now	22.7	24.7	26.8	30.9	29.1
Use it more often than I do now	6.0	7.1	7.4	6.3	6.0
Use it less than I do now	1.3	1.5	1.5	2.7	2.5
Don't know	8.5	8.1	6.6	6.7	6.1

Source: National Institute on Drug Abuse

Trends in Seniors' Attitudes Toward Marijuana Laws

(Entries in percentages)

Class of 1980	Class of 1981	Class of 1982	Class of 1983	Class of 1984	Class of 1985	Class of 1986	Class of 1987	Class of 1988	Class of 1989
26.3	23.1	20.0	18.9	18.6	16.6	14.9	15.4	15.1	16.6
30.9	29.3	28.2	26.3	23.6	25.7	25.9	24.8	21.9	18.9
26.4	32.1	34.7	36.7	40.6	40.8	42.5	45.3	49.2	50.0
16.4	15.4	17.1	18.1	17.2	16.9	16.7	14.8	13.9	14.8
25.0	27.7	29.3	27.4	30.9	32.6	33.0	36.0	36.8	38.8
51.8	48.6	46.2	47.6	45.8	43.2	42.2	41.2	39.0	37.9
9.6	10.5	10.7	10.5	10.6	11.2	10.4	9.2	10.5	9.2
13.6	13.2	13.8	14.6	12.8	13.1	14.4	13.6	12.8	14.1
53.3	55.2	60.0	60.1	62.0	63.0	62.4	64.9	69.0	70.1
6.8	6.0	6.3	7.2	6.6	7.5	7.6	7.3	7.1	8.7
27.3	24.8	21.7	19.8	19.1	17.7	16.8	16.2	13.1	13.0
4.2	4.7	3.8	4.9	4.7	3.7	5.0	4.1	4.3	2.4
2.6	2.5	2.2	1.5	1.6	1.6	2.0	1.3	1.5	2.1
5.9	6.9	6.0	6.4	6.0	6.5	6.1	6.3	5.0	5.7

is most successful when combined with other primary and secondary prevention activities.

In addition, capitalizing on the fact that preteen and teenage attitudes toward drugs are strongly influenced by peers, some prevention programs are led by young people themselves. Yearly repetition of drug education information as students progress from grade to grade has also proven valuable. A Cornell University study, for example, found reduced tobacco, alcohol, and marijuana use when a peer-led program in seventh grade was followed by a "booster" education program in eighth grade.

Drug education and prevention programs also appear to be more effective when parents become involved. Moreover, some studies indicate that female students often respond well to teacher intervention, whereas male students, who may have more difficulty dealing with those in authority, generally do not.

Media campaigns, such as the Partnership for a Drug-Free America, aim to shape attitudes toward drug use through print and television advertising. Although some research has

A police officer visits a Miami elementary school classroom as part of a local drug education program.

found these programs successful (see Chapter 4), it remains to be seen just how effective the mass media are in changing attitudes regarding drug use.

Treatment

Outside support can be beneficial for individuals trying to break marijuana dependence. Individual and group psychotherapy can help individuals learn to reduce the stresses that contributed to dependence; to increase self-esteem; and to work toward making their life more productive and satisfying. Substance abuse treatment for teenagers often includes educational and vocational counseling, family therapy, and participation in organized activities. Though in exceptional cases treatment for marijuana dependence may take place in a hospital or short-term residential treatment center, generally it is conducted on an outpatient basis.

Some individuals enter treatment programs for marijuana dependence voluntarily. Others are referred to treatment programs by parents, doctors, the legal system, teachers, or employers. *Employee Assistance Programs* (EAPs) within businesses are beginning to offer employees with substance abuse problems referrals to therapists and treatment agencies. Many EAPs even offer their own counseling.

As mentioned earlier, it has been reported that individuals who stop using marijuana abruptly after a period of heavy (daily or almost daily) use can undergo a period of physical discomfort, though it usually runs its course in 48 to 96 hours. Symptoms that occur in varying degrees can include loss of appetite (sometimes leading to weight loss), sleeplessness, hot flashes, irritability, and sweating. More extreme reactions may occur in very heavy users and in those who are taking psychoactive drugs to treat emotional disorders. In some cases, psychiatric help may be needed during withdrawal.

Another treatment option is Potsmokers Anonymous, in which small groups of people meet weekly for approximately nine weeks. Participants discuss why they want to stop using marijuana and work toward a better understanding of themselves and their emotions. In addition, participants learn skills enabling them to cope with stressful situations and enjoy life without relying upon marijuana.

At his Washington, D.C., home, glaucoma patient Robert Randall smokes a marijuana cigarette—legally. Randall was the first person allowed by the federal government to use the drug for medical purposes. Since 1977 he has regularly bought marijuana at a local pharmacy to treat the deadly eye disease, which can cause blindness.

CHAPTER 7

MARIJUANA: THE FUTURE

Clearly, many questions concerning marijuana remain unanswered, including the true effects of both occasional and long-term use, as well as the drug's potential medical applications. Future research in these areas may accompany a reevaluation of the cannabis plant as a potential agricultural resource. Current policy, a curious blend of aggressive rhetoric and ambivalent law enforcement, may be similarily reexamined as the overall drug problem grows larger, court systems become more overcrowded, and police and education budgets become strained.

Marijuana as Medicine
When large-scale research into the effects of marijuana began in the early 1970s, the issue of marijuana's potential as a medicinal substance was revived as both old and new uses were discussed. Perhaps the foremost recognized medical use for marijuana is to combat the nausea and loss of appetite that generally accompany cancer chemotherapy, as well as to battle these same symptoms in persons suffering from AIDS. In fact, a recent study by Harvard University found that among more than 1,000 cancer specialists surveyed, almost half said that they would prescribe the drug to patients if it were legal. Moreover, almost as many admitted that they had already recommended marijuana to patients, despite the drug's illegal status. Because of its tendency to enhance ap-

petite, marijuana may also hold promise in treating persons suffering from the eating disorder known as anorexia nervosa.

In addition, the drug has been found useful in treating some patients suffering from glaucoma, a common eye disease in which increased pressure in the eye damages the optic nerve and can eventually cause blindness. Smoking or eating marijuana helps reduce this pressure, and some glaucoma sufferers find marijuana preferable to other available drugs in terms of its effectiveness and relative lack of unpleasant side effects.

Marijuana has also shown some promise as a treatment for asthma. The drug opens bronchial passages in the lungs, allowing some patients to breathe more freely. For similar reasons, moderate use of marijuana may prove effective in treating emphysema sufferers. In certain cases, however, mar-

A pharmacist prepares marijuana tablets in a research laboratory at Mt. Sinai Hospital in New York City. Although the synthetic THC pill was developed for medical purposes, some studies indicate that THC derived directly from the cannabis plant is more effective and has fewer side effects than the synthetic product.

ijuana smoke may irritate the lungs, counteracting some of the benefits of such treatment. Moreover, a 1987 study by the UCLA School of Medicine confirmed reports that marijuana use decreased spasticity (uncontrollable muscle spasms) in patients suffering from multiple sclerosis and suggested there may be a role for THC in treating the disease.

Research at the Medical College of Virginia suggests that in certain cases marijuana use can interfere with the growth of tumors. Marijuana has also been considered for use in reducing stress and muscular tension, relieving migraine headaches, and treating depression. In addition, the drug has been shown to have some painkilling abilities when applied as a plaster or ointment. (Such marijuana preparations were commonly sold as patent medicines from the 1800s through the 1930s.)

Medical Use Dilemma

However, medical use of the drug remains problematic. Since 1976, the DEA has consistently rejected bids to make marijuana legal for medical purposes. In 1986, a series of public hearings were held across the nation to take testimony on the drug's medical usefulness. These hearings were presided over by Francis Young, then chief administrative law judge of the DEA. More than 60 affidavits, both endorsing and dismissing marijuana's therapeutic potential, were filed over the course of 2 years. In 1988, Judge Young called marijuana "one of the safest therapeutically active substances known to man" and recommended that the drug be reclassified from Schedule I to Schedule II, an action that would open the doors for its use as medication. However, in 1989, John Lawn, then head of the DEA, declined to reclassify marijuana, and it remains a Schedule I drug—one with no recognized medical use. Another problem regarding the medical use of marijuana involves the complex array of compounds that make up marijuana (only 400 of a suspected 1,000 have been identified). These can vary greatly in proportion from plant to plant, and as a result it could be difficult to determine and standardize dosages of the drug.

Nonetheless, there have been efforts to create artificial substances that duplicate the beneficial effects of natural marijuana. Delta-9 THC, the most active cannabinoid compound in marijuana, was first synthesized in 1964, and since then synthetic forms of THC have been offered for some medical uses. (Roxane Laboratories markets dronabinol, a synthetic form of THC, under the brand name Marinol.) Use of synthesized THC has met with some success in treating nausea and muscle spasms, but some reports indicate that it does not work as well as natural marijuana. In addition, the intoxicating side effects of artificial THC can be far greater than those produced by smoking marijuana.

The Alliance for Cannabis Therapeutics (ACT) was formed in 1981 by Robert Randall, a glaucoma sufferer who set a precedent by petitioning for and earning the right to use marijuana legally to treat his ailment. ACT has lobbied extensively to end the federal prohibition against using marijuana medicinally.

Marijuana plants under cultivation. For a number of years, marijuana has been known to reduce the symptoms associated with glaucoma and to relieve discomfort resulting from chemotherapy. Recent studies suggest that it is also effective in the treatment of migraine headaches, anorexia nervosa (an eating disorder), and multiple sclerosis.

Over the years, some cancer patients, glaucoma sufferers, and more recently AIDS patients have obtained legal marijuana through the government to treat their illnesses. However, the process involved in getting such requests approved is lengthy and difficult: As of 1990, fewer than 10 persons were receiving legal marijuana. Because of this, many patients turn to illicit sources for the drug in order to medicate their symptoms.

Hemp and Ecology

Since the late 1980s, attention has been redirected toward the issue of legalized cannabis by environmental activists, who claim that reviving the plant as a commercial crop would offer a variety of ecologically sound alternatives to conventional resources.

A demonstrator carries a sign claiming benefits for marijuana use at a rally at the University of Wisconsin in Madison in the fall of 1990. Thousands of supporters of marijuana legalization marched to the state capitol during the university's annual Harvest Fest celebration to share their views with legislators.

Paper Proponents cite U.S. government estimates affirming that, if grown for papermaking, cannabis could, over time, produce four times as much paper fiber per acre as tree pulp. (Hemp is still grown widely in many parts of the world for this purpose, notably in Italy and China.) Advocates maintain that hemp fiber and the hemp hurd (the woody portion of the stalk that surrounds the plant fiber) require far fewer polluting chemicals in processing than does wood and would be equivalent if not superior to wood pulp for making all grades of paper and paper products. Further, the rapid decimation of U.S. forest land could be slowed by preserving trees.

Fabric Hemp blends easily with other fibers and can be processed to yield various textures of extremely durable fabric. Used as an alternative fiber source to cotton, hemp is easier to grow and more resistant to disease and predators, thus requiring fewer pesticides and fertilizers. (By some estimates, more than half of the chemicals used in American agriculture are used on cotton.) In addition, cannabis plants are far less damaging to soil than cotton plants.

A Colombian marijuana field. Mexico and Colombia supply most of the marijuana imported into the United States.

Fuel and Food Advocates also promote the cannabis plant's value as a source of methanol, methane, and other fuels. They further note that marijuana seeds, which do not contain the drug's psychoactive chemicals, do possess, after soybeans, the most complete vegetable protein known and therefore could prove valuable as a food. The seed can also be pressed for its oil, which can be used in paints and other products. Many of these ideas are not new but are simply being reclaimed from records of earlier practices that were common before the cannabis plant was outlawed.

Groups such as NORML, the Business Alliance for Commerce in Hemp, Help End Marijuana Prohibition, and the Drug Policy Foundation are among the organizations lobbying for a reevaluation of the cannabis plant. Their effectiveness in countering the negative public opinion surrounding marijuana, however, remains to be seen.

An Uncertain Future

Attitudes in the early 1990s appear to be leaning against marijuana use; however, arguments surrounding the drug, both pro and con, are often one-sided. For those who claim that the substance is harmless, there is strong indication that marijuana use—especially heavy use—presents serious health hazards. On the other hand, its direct connection to the societal problems that have resulted from the abuse of crack, cocaine, and heroin are tenuous.

Do the possible benefits of hemp production—industrial, environmental, and medical—outweigh the problems associated with legalized marijuana? This question, and the many different ways in which Americans perceive the drug, suggest that marijuana use will remain a controversial issue for some time to come.

Appendix I

POPULATION ESTIMATES OF LIFETIME AND CURRENT NONMEDICAL DRUG USE, 1988

	12-17 years (pop. 20,250,000)		18-25 years (pop. 29,688,000)	
	% Ever Used	% Current User	% Ever Used	% Current User
Marijuana & Hashish	17 3,516,000	6 1,296,000	56 16,741,000	16 4,594,000
Hallucinogens	3 704,000	1 168,000	14 4,093,000	2 569,000
Inhalants	9 1,774,000	2 410,000	12 3,707,000	2 514,000
Cocaine	3 683,000	1 225,000	20 5,858,000	5 1,323,000
Crack	1 188,000	+ +	3 1,000,000	1 249,000
Heroin	1 118,000	+ +	+ +	+ +
Stimulants*	4 852,000	1 245,000	1 3,366,000	2 718,000
Sedatives	2 475,000	1 1 23,000	6 1,633,000	1 265,000
Tranquilizers	2 413,000	+ +	8 2,319,000	1 307,000
Analgesics	4 840,000	1 182,000	9 2,798,000	1 440,000
Alcohol	50 10,161,000	25 5,097,000	90 26,807,000	65 19,392,000
Cigarettes	42 8,564,000	12 2,389,000	75 22,251,000	35 10,447,000
Smokeless Tobacco	15 3,021,000	4 722,000	24 6,971,000	6 1,855,000

* Amphetamines and related substances
+ Amounts of less than .5% are not listed
   Terms: Ever Used: used at least once in a person's lifetime.
          Current User: used at least once in the 30 days prior to the survey.

Source: National Institute on Drug Abuse, August 1989

POPULATION ESTIMATES OF LIFETIME AND CURRENT
NONMEDICAL DRUG USE, 1988

	26+ years (pop. 148,409,000)				TOTAL (pop. 198,347,000)		
%	Ever Used	%	Current User	%	Ever Used	%	Current User
31	45,491,000	4	5,727,000	33	65,748,000	6	11,616,000
7	9,810,000	+	+	7	4,607,000	+	+
4	5,781,000	+	+	6	1,262,000	1	1,223,000
10	14,631,000	1	1,375,000	11	21,171,000	2	2,923,000
+	+	+	+	1	2,483,000	+	484,000
1	1,686,000	+	+	1	1,907,000	+	+
7	9,850,000	1	791,000	7	4,068,000	1	1,755,000
3	4,867,000	+	+	4	6,975,000	+	+
5	6,750,000	1	822,000	5	9,482,000	1	1,174,000
5	6,619,000	+	+	5	10,257,000	1	1,151,000
89	131,530,000	55	81,356,000	85	168,498,000	53	105,845,000
80	118,191,000	30	44,284,000	75	149,005,000	29	57,121,000
13	19,475,000	3	4,497,000	15	29,467,000	4	7,073,000

Appendix II

DRUGS MENTIONED MOST FREQUENTLY BY HOSPITAL EMERGENCY ROOMS, 1988

	Drug name	Number of mentions by emergency rooms	Percent of total number of mentions
1	Cocaine	62,141	38.80
2	Alcohol-in-combination	46,588	29.09
3	Heroin/Morphine	20,599	12.86
4	Marijuana/Hashish	10,722	6.69
5	PCP/PCP Combinations	8,403	5.25
6	Acetaminophen	6,426	4.01
7	Diazepam	6,082	3.80
8	Aspirin	5,544	3.46
9	Ibuprofen	3,878	2.42
10	Alprazolam	3,846	2.40
11	Methamphetamine/Speed	3,030	1.89
12	Acetaminophen W Codeine	2,457	1.53
13	Amitriptyline	1,960	1.22
14	D.T.C. Sleep Aids	1,820	1.14
15	Methadone	1,715	1.07
16	Triazolam	1,640	1.02
17	Diphenhydramine	1,574	0.98
18	D-Propoxyphene	1,563	0.98
19	Hydantoin	1,442	0.90
20	Lorazepam	1,345	0.84
21	LSD	1,317	0.82
22	Amphetamine	1,316	0.82
23	Phenobarbital	1,223	0.76
24	Oxycodone	1,192	0.74
25	Imipramine	1,064	0.66

Source: Drug Abuse Warning Network (DAWN), Annual Data 1988

Appendix III

DRUGS MENTIONED MOST FREQUENTLY BY MEDICAL EXAMINERS (IN AUTOPSY REPORTS), 1988

	Drug name	Number of mentions in autopsy reports	Percent of total number of drug mentions
1	Cocaine	3,308	48.96
2	Alcohol-in-combination	2,596	38.43
3	Heroin/Morphine	2,480	36.71
4	Codeine	689	10.20
5	Diazepam	464	6.87
6	Methadone	447	6.62
7	Amitriptyline	402	5.95
8	Nortriptyline	328	4.85
9	Lidocaine	306	4.53
10	Acetaminophen	293	4.34
11	D-Propoxyphene	271	4.01
12	Marijuana/Hashish	263	3.89
13	Quinine	224	3.32
14	Unspec Benzodiazepine	222	3.29
15	PCP/PCP Combinations	209	3.09
16	Diphenhydramine	192	2.84
17	Phenobarbital	183	2.71
18	Desipramine	177	2.62
19	Methamphetamine/Speed	161	2.38
20	Doxepin	152	2.25
21	Aspirin	138	2.04
22	Imipramine	137	2.03
23	Hydantoin	98	1.45
24	Amphetamine	87	1.29
25	Chlordiazepoxide	76	1.12

Source: Drug Abuse Warning Network (DAWN), Annual Data 1988

Appendix IV

NATIONAL HIGH SCHOOL SENIOR SURVEY, 1975-1989

	High School Senior Survey Trends in Lifetime Prevalence Percent Who Ever Used				
	Class of 1975	Class of 1976	Class of 1977	Class of 1978	Class of 1979
Marijuana/Hashish	47.3	52.8	56.4	59.2	60.4
Inhalants	NA	10.3	11.1	12.0	12.7
Inhalants Adjusted	NA	NA	NA	NA	18.2
Amyl & Butyl Nitrites	NA	NA	NA	NA	11.1
Hallucinogens	16.3	15.1	13.9	14.3	14.1
Hallucinogens Adjusted	NA	NA	NA	NA	17.7
LSD	11.3	11.0	9.8	9.7	9.5
PCP	NA	NA	NA	NA	12.8
Cocaine	9.0	9.7	10.8	12.9	15.4
Crack	NA	NA	NA	NA	NA
Other cocaine	NA	NA	NA	NA	NA
Heroin	2.2	1.8	1.8	1.6	1.1
Other Opiates*	9.0	9.6	10.3	9.9	10.1
Stimulants*	22.3	22.6	23.0	22.9	24.2
Stimulants Adjusted*	NA	NA	NA	NA	NA
Sedatives*	18.2	17.7	17.4	16.0	14.6
Barbiturates*	16.9	16.2	15.6	13.7	11.8
Methaqualone*	8.1	7.8	8.5	7.9	8.3
Tranquilizers*	17.0	16.8	18.0	17.0	16.3
Alcohol	90.4	91.9	92.5	93.1	93.0
Cigarettes	73.6	75.4	75.7	75.3	74.0

Stimulants adjusted to exclude inappropriate reporting of nonprescription stimulants; stimulants = amphetamines and amphetamine-like substances.
*Only use not under a doctor's orders included.

Source: National Institute on Drug Abuse, National High School Senior Survey: "Monitoring the Future," 1989

High School Senior Survey
Trends in Lifetime Prevalence
Percent Who Ever Used

Class of 1980	Class of 1981	Class of 1982	Class of 1983	Class of 1984	Class of 1985	Class of 1986	Class of 1987	Class of 1988	Class of 1989
60.3	59.5	58.7	57.0	54.9	54.2	50.9	50.2	47.2	43.7
11.9	12.3	12.8	13.6	14.4	15.4	15.9	17.0	16.7	17.6
17.3	17.2	17.7	18.2	18.0	18.1	20.1	18.6	17.5	18.6
11.1	10.1	9.8	8.4	8.1	7.9	8.6	4.7	3.2	3.3
13.3	13.3	12.5	11.9	10.7	10.3	9.7	10.3	8.9	9.4
15.6	15.3	14.3	13.6	12.3	12.1	11.9	10.6	9.2	9.9
9.3	9.8	9.6	8.9	8.0	7.5	7.2	8.4	7.7	8.3
9.6	7.8	6.0	5.6	5.0	4.9	4.8	3.0	2.9	3.9
15.7	16.5	16.0	16.2	16.1	17.3	16.9	15.2	12.1	10.3
NA	NA	NA	NA	NA	NA	NA	5.4	4.8	4.7
NA	NA	NA	NA	NA	NA	NA	14.0	12.1	8.5
1.1	1.1	1.2	1.2	1.3	1.2	1.1	1.2	1.1	1.3
9.8	10.1	9.6	9.4	9.7	10.2	9.0	9.2	8.6	8.3
26.4	32.2	35.6	35.4	NA	NA	NA	NA	NA	NA
NA	NA	27.9	26.9	27.9	26.2	23.4	21.6	19.8	19.1
14.9	16.0	15.2	14.4	13.3	11.8	10.4	8.7	7.8	7.4
11.0	11.3	10.3	9.9	9.9	9.2	8.4	7.4	6.7	6.5
9.5	10.6	10.7	10.1	8.3	6.7	5.2	4.0	3.3	2.7
15.2	14.7	14.0	13.3	12.4	11.9	10.9	10.9	9.4	7.6
93.2	92.6	92.8	92.6	92.6	92.2	91.3	92.2	92.0	90.7
71.0	71.0	70.1	70.6	69.7	68.8	67.6	67.2	66.4	65.7

Appendix V

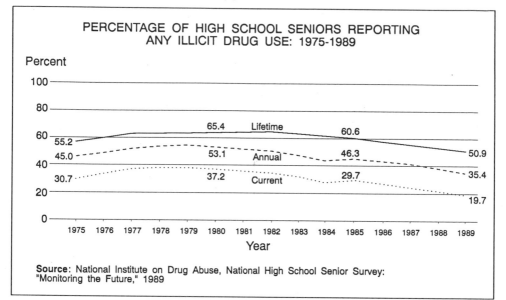

PERCENTAGE OF HIGH SCHOOL SENIORS REPORTING
ANY ILLICIT DRUG USE: 1975-1989

Percent

100			
80			
60	55.2	65.4 Lifetime	60.6
	45.0	53.1 Annual	46.3 — 50.9
40			
	30.7	37.2 Current	29.7 — 35.4
20			
			19.7
0			

1975 1976 1977 1978 1979 1980 1981 1982 1983 1984 1985 1986 1987 1988 1989

Year

Source: National Institute on Drug Abuse, National High School Senior Survey: "Monitoring the Future," 1989

Appendix VI

DRUG ABUSE AND AIDS

An estimated 25 percent of all cases of acquired immunodeficiency syndrome, or AIDS, are intravenous (IV) drug abusers. This group is the second largest at risk for AIDS, exceeded only by homosexual, and bisexual men. And the numbers may be growing. Data for the first half of 1988 show that IV drug abusers made up about 31 percent of the total reported cases.

". . . the number of IV drug users with AIDS is doubling every 14-16 months."

According to the National Institute on Drug Abuse (NIDA). There are 1.1 to 1.3 million IV drug users in the United States, and, so far, about 17,500 have developed AIDS. Thousands more are infected with the virus that causes this fatal illness, which kills by destroying the body's ability to fight disease.

Currently, the number of IV drug users with AIDS is doubling every 14-16 months. Although the numbers of IV drug users who carry the AIDS virus varies from region to region, in some places the majority may already be infected. In New York City, for example, 60 percent of IV drug users entering treatment programs have the AIDS virus.

Among IV drug abusers, the AIDS virus is spread primarily by needle sharing. As long as IV drug abusers are drug dependent, they are likely to engage in needle sharing. Thus, the key to eliminating needle sharing—and the associated spread of AIDS—is drug abuse treatment to curb drug dependence. NIDA is working to find ways to get more IV users into treatment and to develop new methods to fight drug addiction. Most non-drug users characteristically associate heroin with IV drug use. However, thousands of others inject cocaine or amphetamines. Recent evidence suggests that IV cocaine use is increasing and that the AIDS virus is spreading in those users. One reason for this may be because cocaine's effects last only a short time. When the drug, which is a stimulant, wears off, users may inject again and again, sharing a needle many times in a few hours. In contrast, heroin users inject once and fall asleep.

". . . IV cocaine use is increasing and the AIDS virus is spreading in those users."

The apparent increase in IV cocaine is especially worrisome, drug abuse experts say, because there are no standard therapies for treating cocaine addiction. Until scientists find effective treatments for this problem, the ability to control the spread of AIDS will be hampered.

TRANSMISSION

Needle Sharing -- Among IV drug users, transmission of AIDS virus most often occurs by sharing needles, syringes, or other "works." Small amounts of contaminated blood left in the equipment can carry the virus from user to user. IV drug abusers who frequent "shooting galleries" — where paraphernalia is passed among several people -- are at especially high risk for AIDS. But, needle sharing of any sort (at parties, for example) can transmit the virus, and NIDA experts note that almost all IV drug users share needles at one time or another.
Because not every IV drug abuser will enter treatment and because some must wait to be treated, IV users in many cities are being taught to flush their "works" with bleach before they inject. Used correctly, bleach can destroy virus left in the equipment.

Sexual Transmission -- IV drug abusers also get AIDS through unprotected sex with someone who is infected. In addition, the AIDS virus can be sexually transmitted from infected IV drug abusers to individuals who do not use drugs. Data from the Centers for Disease Control show that IV drug use is associated with the increased spread of AIDS in the heterosexual population. For example, of all women reported to have AIDS, 49 percent were IV drug users, while another 30 percent -- non-IV drug users themselves -- were sexual partners of IV drug users. Infected women who become pregnant can pass the AIDS virus to their babies. About 70 percent of all children born with AIDS have had a mother or father who shot drugs.

Non-IV Drug Use and AIDS -- Sexual activity has also been reported as the means of AIDS transmission among those who use non-IV drugs (like crack or marijuana). Many people, especially women, addicted to crack (or other substances) go broke supporting their habit and turn to trading sex for drugs. Another link between substance abuse and AIDS is when individuals using alcohol and drugs relax their restraints and caution regarding sexual behavior. People who normally practice "safe" sex may neglect to do so while "under the influence."

Source: U.S. Public Health Service, AIDS Program Office, 1989

Appendix VII

U.S. Drug Schedules*

	Drugs Included	Dispensing Regulations
Schedule I high potential for abuse; no currently accepted medical use in treatment in U.S.; safety not proven for medical use	heroin methaqualone LSD mescaline peyote phencyclidine analogs psilocybin marijuana hashish	research use only
Schedule II high potential for abuse; currently accepted U.S. medical use; abuse may lead to severe psychological or physical dependence	opium morphine methadone barbiturates cocaine amphetamines phencyclidine codeine	written Rx; no refills
Schedule III less potential for abuse than drugs in Schedules I and II; currently accepted U.S. medical use; may lead to moderate or low physical dependence or high psychological dependence	glutethimide selected morphine, opium, and codeine compounds selected depressant sedative compounds selected stimulants for weight control	written or oral Rx; refills allowed
Schedule IV low potential for abuse relative to drugs in Schedule III; currently accepted U.S. medical use; abuse may lead to limited physical dependence or psychological dependence relative to drugs in Schedule III	selected barbiturate and other depressant compounds selected stimulants for weight control	written or oral Rx; refills allowed
Schedule V low potential for abuse relative to drugs in Schedule IV; currently accepted U.S. medical use; abuse may lead to limited physical dependence or psychological dependence relative to drugs in Schedule IV	selected narcotic compounds	OTC/ M.D.'s order

*Established by the U.S. Controlled Substances Act of 1970
Source: U.S. Drug Enforcement Administration

Appendix VIII

Agencies for the Prevention and Treatment of Drug Abuse

Alabama
Department of Mental Health
Division of Substance Abuse
200 Interstate Park Drive
P.O. Box 3710
Montgomery, AL 36109
(205) 270-9650

Alaska
Department of Health and
  Social Services
Division of Alcoholism and
  Drug Abuse
P.O. Box H
Juneau, AK 99811-0607
(907) 586-6201

Arizona
Department of Health
  Services
Division of Behavioral Health
  Services
Bureau of Community
  Services
The Office of Substance
  Abuse
2632 East Thomas
Phoenix, AZ 85016
(602) 255-1030

Arkansas
Department of Human
  Services
Division of Alcohol and Drug
  Abuse
400 Donagy Plaza North
P.O. Box 1437
Slot 2400
Little Rock, AR 72203-1437
(501) 682-6656

California
Health and Welfare Agencies
Department of Alcohol and
  Drug Programs

1700 K Street
Sacramento, CA 95814-4037
(916) 445-1943

Colorado
Department of Health
Alcohol and Drug Abuse
  Division
4210 East 11th Avenue
Denver, CO 80220
(303) 331-8201

Connecticut
Alcohol and Drug Abuse
  Commission
999 Asylum Avenue
3rd Floor
Hartford, CT 06105
(203) 566-4145

Delaware
Division of Mental Health
Bureau of Alcoholism and
  Drug Abuse
1901 North Dupont Highway
Newcastle, DE 19720
(302) 421-6101

District of Columbia
Department of Human
  Services
Office of Health Planning and
  Development
1660 L Street NW
Room 715
Washington, DC 20036
(202) 724-5641

Florida
Department of Health and
  Rehabilitative Services
Alcohol, Drug Abuse, and
  Mental Health Office
1317 Winewood Boulevard
Building 6, Room 183
Tallahassee, FL 32399-0700
(904) 488-8304

Georgia
Department of Human
  Resources
Division of Mental Health,
  Mental Retardation, and
  Substance Abuse
Alcohol and Drug Section
878 Peachtree Street
Suite 319
Atlanta, GA 30309-3917
(404) 894-4785

Hawaii
Department of Health
Mental Health Division
Alcohol and Drug Abuse
  Branch
1270 Queen Emma Street
Room 706
Honolulu, HI 96813
(808) 548-4280

Idaho
Department of Health and
  Welfare
Bureau of Preventive
  Medicine
Substance Abuse Section
450 West State
Boise, ID 83720
(208) 334-5934

Illinois
Department of Alcoholism
  and Substance Abuse
Illinois Center
100 West Randolph Street
Suite 5-600
Chicago, IL 60601
(312) 814-3840

Indiana
Department of Mental Health
Division of Addiction Services
117 East Washington Street
Indianapolis, IN 46204-3647
(317) 232-7816

Iowa
Department of Public Health
Division of Substance Abuse
Lucas State Office Building
321 East 12th Street
Des Moines, IA 50319
(515) 281-3641

Kansas
Department of Social
  Rehabilitation
Alcohol and Drug Abuse
  Services
300 SW Oakley
2nd Floor
Biddle Building
Topeka, KS 66606
(913) 296-3925

Kentucky
Cabinet for Human Resources
Department of Health
  Services
Substance Abuse Branch
275 East Main Street
Frankfort, KY 40621
(502) 564-2880

Louisiana
Department of Health and
  Hospitals
Office of Human Services
Division of Alcohol and Drug
  Abuse
P.O. Box 3868
Baton Rouge, LA 70821-3868
1201 Capital Access Road
Baton Rouge, LA 70802
(504) 342-9354

Maine
Department of Human
  Services
Office of Alcoholism and
  Drug Abuse Prevention
Bureau of Rehabilitation
5 Anthony Avenue
State House, Station 11
Augusta, ME 04433
(207) 289-2781

Maryland
Alcohol and Drug Abuse
  Administration
201 West Preston Street

4th Floor
Baltimore, MD 21201
(301) 225-6910

Massachusetts
Department of Public Health
Division of Substance Abuse
150 Tremont Street
Boston, MA 02111
(617) 727-1960

Michigan
Department of Public Health
Office of Substance Abuse
  Services
2150 Apollo Drive
P.O. Box 30206
Lansing, MI 48909
(517) 335-8810

Minnesota
Department of Human
  Services
Chemical Dependency
  Division
444 Lafayette Road
St. Paul, MN 55155
(612) 296-4614

Mississippi
Department of Mental Health
Division of Alcohol and Drug
  Abuse
1101 Robert E. Lee Building
239 North Lamar Street
Jackson, MS 39201
(601) 359-1288

Missouri
Department of Mental
  Health
Division of Alcoholism and
  Drug Abuse
1706 East Elm Street
P.O. Box 687
Jefferson City, MO 65102
(314) 751-4942

Montana
Department of Institutions
Alcohol and Drug Abuse
  Division
1539 11th Avenue
Helena, MT 59620
(406) 444-2827

Nebraska
Department of Public
  Institutions
Division of Alcoholism and
  Drug Abuse
801 West Van Dorn Street
P.O. Box 94728
Lincoln, NB 68509-4728
(402) 471-2851, Ext. 5583

Nevada
Department of Human
  Resources
Bureau of Alcohol and Drug
  Abuse
505 East King Street
Room 500
Carson City, NV 89710
(702) 687-4790

New Hampshire
Department of Health and
  Human Services
Office of Alcohol and Drug
  Abuse Prevention
State Office
Park South
105 Pleasant Street
Concord, NH 03301
(603) 271-6100

New Jersey
Department of Health
Division of Alcoholism and
  Drug Abuse
129 East Hanover Street CN
362
Trenton, NJ 08625
(609) 292-8949

New Mexico
Health and Environment
  Department
Behavioral Health Services
  Division/
Substance Abuse
Harold Runnels Building
1190 Saint Francis Drive
Santa Fe, NM 87503
(505) 827-2601

New York
Division of Alcoholism and
  Alcohol Abuse
194 Washington Avenue

Albany, NY 12210
(518) 474-5417

Division of Substance Abuse
  Services
Executive Park South
Box 8200
Albany, NY 12203
(518) 457-7629

North Carolina
Department of Human
  Resources
Division of Mental Health,
  Developmental Disabilities,
  and Substance Abuse
  Services
Alcohol and Drug Abuse
  Services
325 North Salisbury Street
Albemarle Building
Raleigh, NC 27603
(919) 733-4670

North Dakota
Department of Human Services
Division of Alcohol and Drug
  Abuse
1839 East Capital Avenue
Bismarck, ND 58501-2152
(701) 224-2769

Ohio
Division of Alcohol and Drug
  Addiction Services
246 North High Street
3rd Floor
Columbus, OH 43266-0170
(614) 466-3445

Oklahoma
Department of Mental Health
  and Substance Abuse
  Services
Alcohol and Drug Abuse
  Services
1200 North East 13th Street
P.O. Box 53277
Oklahoma City, OK 73152-
  3277
(405) 271-8653

Oregon
Department of Human
  Resources

Office of Alcohol and Drug
  Abuse Programs
1178 Chemeketa NE
#102
Salem, OR 97310
(503) 378-2163

Pennsylvania
Department of Health
Office of Drug and Alcohol
  Programs
Health and Welfare Building
Room 809
P.O. Box 90
Harrisburg, PA 17108
(717) 787-9857

Rhode Island
Department of Mental Health,
  Mental Retardation and
  Hospitals
Division of Substance Abuse
Substance Abuse
  Administration Building
P.O. Box 20363
Cranston, RI 02920
(401) 464-2091

South Carolina
Commission on Alcohol and
  Drug Abuse
3700 Forest Drive
Suite 300
Columbia, SC 29204
(803) 734-9520

South Dakota
Department of Human Services
700 Governor's Drive
Pier South D
Pierre, SD 57501-2291
(605) 773-4806

Tennessee
Department of Mental Health
  and Mental Retardation
Alcohol and Drug Abuse
  Services
706 Church Street
Nashville, TN 37243-0675
(615) 741-1921

Texas
Commission on Alcohol and
  Drug Abuse

720 Bracos Street
Suite 403
Austin, TX 78701
(512) 463-5510

Utah
Department of Social Services
Division of Substance Abuse
120 North 200 West
4th Floor
Salt Lake City, UT 84103
(801) 538-3939

Vermont
Agency of Human Services
Department of Social and
  Rehabilitation Services
Office of Alcohol and Drug
  Abuse Programs
103 South Main Street
Waterbury, VT 05676
(802) 241-2170

Virginia
Department of Mental Health
  and Mental Retardation
Division of Substance Abuse
109 Governor Street
8th Floor
P.O. Box 1797
Richmond, VA 23214
(804) 786-5313

Washington
Department of Social and
  Health Service
Division of Alcohol and
  Substance Abuse
12th and Franklin
Mail Stop OB 21W
Olympia, WA 98504
(206) 753-5866

West Virginia
Department of Health and
  Human Resources
Office of Behavioral Health
  Services
Division on Alcoholism and
  Drug Abuse
Capital Complex
1900 Kanawha Boulevard East
Building 3, Room 402
Charleston, WV 25305
(304) 348-2276

Wisconsin
Department of Health and
Social Services
Division of Community
Services
Bureau of Community
Programs
Office of Alcohol and Drug
Abuse
1 West Wilson Street
P.O. Box 7851
Madison, WI 53707-7851
(608) 266-2717

Wyoming
Alcohol And Drug Abuse
Programs
451 Hathaway Building
Cheyenne, WY 82002
(307) 777-7115

U.S. TERRITORIES AND POSSESSIONS

American Samoa
LBJ Tropical Medical Center
Department of Mental Health
Clinic
Pago Pago, American Samoa
96799

Guam
Mental Health & Substance
Abuse Agency
P.O. Box 20999
Guam 96921

Puerto Rico
Department of Addiction
Control Services
Alcohol and Drug Abuse
Programs
Avenida Barbosa
P.O. Box 414
Rio Piedras, PR 00928-1474
(809) 763-7575

Trust Territories
Director of Health Services
Office of the High
Commissioner
Saipan, Trust Territories
96950

Virgin Islands
Division of Health and
Substance Abuse
Becastro Building
3rd Street, Sugar Estate
St. Thomas, Virgin Islands
00802

CANADA

Canadian Centre on
Substance Abuse
112 Kent Street, Suite 480
Ottawa, Ontario
K1P 5P2
(613) 235-4048

Alberta
Alberta Alcohol and Drug
Abuse Commission
10909 Jasper Avenue, 6th
Floor
Edmonton, Alberta
T5J 3M9
(403) 427-2837

British Columbia
Ministry of Labour and
Consumer Services
Alcohol and Drug Programs
1019 Wharf Street, 5th Floor
Victoria, British Columbia
V8V 1X4
(604) 387-5870

Manitoba
The Alcoholism Foundation of
Manitoba
1031 Portage Avenue
Winnipeg, Manitoba
R3G 0R8
(204) 944-6226

New Brunswick
Alcoholism and Drug
Dependency Commission
of New Brunswick
65 Brunswick Street
P.O. Box 6000
Fredericton, New Brunswick
E3B 5H1
(506) 453-2136

Newfoundland
The Alcohol and Drug
Dependency Commission
of Newfoundland and
Labrador
Suite 105, Prince Charles
Building
120 Torbay Road, 1st Floor
St. John's, Newfoundland
A1A 2G8
(709) 737-3600

Northwest Territories
Alcohol and Drug Services
Department of Social Services
Government of Northwest
Territories
Box 1320 - 52nd Street
6th Floor, Precambrian
Building
Yellowknife, Northwest
Territories
S1A 2L9
(403) 920-8005

Nova Scotia
Nova Scotia Commission on
Drug Dependency
6th Floor, Lord Nelson
Building
5675 Spring Garden Road
Halifax, Nova Scotia
B3J 1H1
(902) 424-4270

Ontario
Addiction Research
Foundation
33 Russell Street
Toronto, Ontario
M5S 2S1
(416) 595-6000

Prince Edward Island
Addiction Services of Prince
Edward Island
P.O. Box 37
Eric Found Building
65 McGill Avenue
Charlottetown, Prince Edward
Island
C1A 7K2
(902) 368-4120

Quebec

Service des Programmes aux
    Personnes Toxicomanie
Gouvernement du Quebec
Ministere de la Sante et des
    Services Sociaux
1005 Chemin Ste. Foy
Quebec City, Quebec
G1S 4N4
(418) 643-9887

Saskatchewan

Saskatchewan Alcohol and
    Drug Abuse Commission
1942 Hamilton Street
Regina, Saskatchewan
S4P 3V7
(306) 787-4085

Yukon

Alcohol and Drug Services
Department of Health and
    Social Resources
Yukon Territorial
    Government
6118-6th Avenue
P.O. Box 2703
Whitehorse, Yukon Territory
Y1A 2C6
(403) 667-5777

Further Reading

General

Berger, Gilda. *Drug Abuse: The Impact on Society*. New York: Watts, 1988. (Gr. 7–12)

Cohen, Susan, and Daniel Cohen. *What You Can Believe About Drugs: An Honest and Unhysterical Guide for Teens*. New York: M. Evans, 1987. (Gr. 7–12)

Musto, David F. *The American Disease: Origins of Narcotic Control*. Rev. ed. New Haven: Yale University Press, 1987.

National Institute on Drug Abuse. *Drug Use, Drinking, and Smoking: National Survey Results from High School, College, and Young Adult Populations, 1975–1988*. Washington, DC: Public Health Service, Department of Health and Human Services, 1989.

O'Brien, Robert, and Sidney Cohen. *Encyclopedia of Drug Abuse*. New York: Facts on File, 1984.

Snyder, Solomon H., M.D. *Drugs and the Brain*. New York: Scientific American Books, 1986.

U.S. Department of Justice. *Drugs of Abuse*. 1989 ed. Washington, DC: Government Printing Office, 1989.

Marijuana

Abel, Ernest L. *A Marihuana Dictionary: Words, Terms, Events, and Persons Relating to Cannabis*. Westport, CT: Greenwood Press, 1982.

———. *Marihuana: The First Twelve Thousand Years*. New York: Plenum Press, 1980.

Hending, Herbert, et al. *Living High: Daily Marijuana Use Among Adults*. New York: Human Sciences Press, 1987.

Himmelstein, Jerome L. *The Strange Career of Marijuana: Politics and Ideology of Drug Control in America*. Westport, CT: Greenwood Press, 1983.

Kleiman, Mark A. R. *Marijuana: Costs of Abuse, Costs of Control.* Westport, CT: Greenwood Press, 1989.

"Marijuana Use and Memory Loss." *American Family Physician*, March 1990.

Glossary

acetylcholine a chemical in the brain that transmits signals from one brain cell to another; marijuana can impair short-term memory by inhibiting the release of acetylcholine

AIDS acquired immune deficiency syndrome; an acquired defect in the immune system; the final stage of the disease caused by the human immunodeficiency virus (HIV); spread by the exchange of blood (including contaminated hypodermic needles), by sexual contact, through nutritive fluids passed from a mother to her fetus, and through breast-feeding; leaves victims vulnerable to certain, often fatal, infections and cancers

amotivational syndrome a loss of motivation in an individual, accompanied by apathy and diminished physical activity

anorexia nervosa a disorder occurring primarily among female adolescents and characterized by a pathological fear of weight gain and often excessive weight loss

aspergillus any fungi of the *Aspergillus* genus; aspergillus fungi are sometimes found in marijuana and can cause lung infections in pot smokers

bong a water pipe sometimes used to smoke marijuana

cannabinoids a number of chemical compounds found only in marijuana; these include THC, cannabidiol, and cannabinol

Cannabis the genus of the Indian hemp plant, *Cannabis sativa*, the source of marijuana as well as various fibers, foods, and oils; the word *cannabis* also refers to any psychoactive substances derived from hemp, including marijuana, hashish, and THC

chemotherapy the use of chemical agents in the treatment or control of disease or mental illness

cocaine a potent stimulant derived from the leaves of the coca plant; usually sold as a powder compound called cocaine hydrochloride

crack a solid form of cocaine hydrochloride in the form of small chips, chunks, or "rocks" that are smoked in a small pipe

delta-9 tetrahydrocannabinol see *THC*

ditchweed a low-potency, wild-growing form of cannabis

dronabinol a synthetic form of THC, marketed under the brand name Marinol and used in the treatment of nausea and muscle spasms

gateway drug a relatively weak drug whose use may lead to experimentation with stronger substances; marijuana is thought by many to be a gateway drug, though this has not been proved *glaucoma* an eye disease characterized by increased pressure in the eyeball and resulting damage to the optic nerve; if untreated it can eventually lead to blindness

gynecomastia excessive development of the male breast, sometimes a consequence of heavy marijuana smoking

hashish a puttylike material derived from cannabis plants that can be smoked in pipes or eaten; also known as *hash*

head shop a store devoted specifically to drug paraphernalia and other items linked to the drug culture

hemp see *Cannabis*

herbicide an agent used to destroy or inhibit plant growth

heroin an addictive, synthetic narcotic that is derived from morphine and used illicitly for its euphoric effects

hookah a water pipe, sometimes used to smoke marijuana

joint a marijuana cigarette

hydroponic describing a plant grown in water rather than soil

leukemia a disease characterized by an abnormal increase in the number of white blood cells

migraine headache a severe, recurrent headache often accompanied by nausea and vomiting; also called *migraine*

multiple sclerosis a progressive disease of the nervous system marked by patches of hardened tissue in the brain or spinal cord, muscle tremors, and partial or complete paralysis

paraquat an herbicide used against marijuana plants; paraquat is highly toxic to humans

PCP phencyclidine, a synthetic hallucinogen; also known as angel dust and crystal

pharmacopeia a book usually issued by an officially recognized authority that describes drugs and other medicinal preparations, and sets forth standards for their preparation; the *United States Pharmacopeia*, for example, is issued by the U.S. government

psychoactive affecting the mind or behavior

retting the process of soaking fiber from woody plant tissue, as in the separation of hemp fibers from the stem of the cannabis plant

roach clips devices for holding marijuana cigarettes

roach stones same as *roach clips*

salmonella any bacteria of the *Salmonella* genus; can cause food poisoning and other digestive disorders as well as various genital diseases

sinsemilla   literally, "without seeds"; marijuana from the female cannabis plant that has not been fertilized by the male plant and therefore does not produce seeds; also known as *sinse*

spliff   a marijuana cigarette

testosterone   a male sex hormone; research indicates that it may be decreased by heavy marijuana smoking

THC   delta-9 tetrahydrocannabinol, the cannabinoid most responsible for the "high" produced by marijuana

Index

William J. Hermes is a teacher and a freelance writer who has developed substance abuse educational materials for the New York City Board of Education and the New York State Division of Substance Abuse Services. He received a bachelor's degree in English from the State University of New York at Binghamton and a master's degree in education from Queens College in New York.

Anne Galperin is the author of several books on health and the environment and previously served as an associate editor at Macmillan Publishing Company. She received a bachelor's degree in human development and social policy from Northwestern University.

Paul R. Sanberg, Ph.D., is a professor of psychiatry, psychology, neurosurgery, physiology, and biophysics at the University of Cincinnati College of Medicine. Currently, he is also a professor of psychiatry at Brown University and scientific director for Cellular Transplants, Inc., in Providence, Rhode Island.

Professor Sanberg has held research positions at the Australian National University at Canberra, the Johns Hopkins University School of Medicine, and Ohio University. He has written many journal articles and book chapters in the fields of neuroscience and psychopharmacology. He has served on the editorial boards of many scientific journals and is the recipient of numerous awards.

Solomon H. Snyder, M.D., is Distinguished Service Professor of Neuroscience, Pharmacology and Psychiatry at the Johns Hopkins University School of Medicine. He has served as president of the Society for Neuroscience and in 1978 received the Albert Lasker Award in Medical Research. He has authored *Drugs and the Brain, Uses of Marijuana, Madness and the Brain, The Troubled Mind*, and *Biological Aspects of Mental Disorder* and has edited *Perspectives in Neuropharmacology: A Tribute to Julius Axelrod*. Professor Snyder was a research associate with Dr. Axelrod at the National Institutes of Health.

Barry L. Jacobs, Ph.D., is currently a professor in the neuroscience program at Princeton University. Professor Jacobs is the author of *Serotonin Neurotransmission and Behavior* and *Hallucinogens: Neurochemical, Behavioral and Clinical Perspectives*. He has written many journal articles in the field of neuroscience and contributed numerous chapters to books on behavior and brain science. He has been a member of several panels of the National Institute of Mental Health.

Jerome H. Jaffe, M.D., formerly professor of psychiatry at the College of Physicians and Surgeons, Columbia University, is director of the Addiction Research Center of the National Institute on Drug Abuse. Dr. Jaffe is also a psychopharmacologist and has conducted research on a wide range of addictive drugs and developed treatment programs for addicts. He has acted as special consultant to the president on narcotics and dangerous drugs and was the first director of the White House Special Action Office for Drug Abuse Prevention.